Blessed Is . . .

Untying the 'Nots' That Hinder Your Blessing

Blessed Is . . .

Untying the 'Nots' That Hinder Your Blessing

Kenneth Hagin Jr.

Unless otherwise indicated, all Scripture quotations in this volume are from the *King James Version* of the Bible.

First Printing 1997

ISBN 0-89276-736-7

In the U.S. write:
Kenneth Hagin Ministries
P.O. Box 50126
Tulsa, OK 74150-0126

In Canada write:
Kenneth Hagin Ministries
P.O. Box 335, Station D,
Etobicoke (Toronto), Ontario
Canada, M9A 4X3

Contents

Chapter 1
What Not *To Do To Be Blessed!*

> *Blessed is the man that WALKETH NOT in the counsel of the ungodly, nor standeth in the way of sinners, nor sitteth in the seat of the scornful.*
>
> *But his delight is in the law of the Lord; and in his law doth he meditate day and night.*
>
> *And he shall be like a tree planted by the rivers of water, that bringeth forth his fruit in his season; his leaf also shall not wither; and whatsoever he doeth shall prosper.*
>
> — Psalm 1:1-3

It seems people are always looking for a quick way to success. For example, have you ever seen an advertisement or a book that had something to do with a quick scheme to make you a success in life? Many people are gullible enough to buy those books, tapes, or other materials that supposedly guarantee success. Why do people buy these materials? Because they're interested in being successful!

Years ago, a book was written about how to dress in a way that exemplified success, and millions of people bought that book. It was a reputable book, and not long after it was published, you could see business people walking down the streets in big cities wearing the same style of clothing. They were all dressing for success!

Most people want to be successful in life. I don't know anyone who *wants* to be a failure. But do you know that the best place to find out how to be successful is in one of the oldest books in the world? This book has been a best-seller for hundreds of years. I'm talking about the Bible.

The answer to success in life comes from the Bible! Yet so many people look everywhere else for success, only to find disappointment. But there's really only one way to be truly successful in life, and that's God's way!

Look again at verse 1 of our text.

> **PSALM 1:1**
> **1 Blessed is the man** [or woman] **that walketh not in the counsel of the ungodly, nor standeth in the way of sinners, nor sitteth in the seat of the scornful.**

I want you to notice that this verse starts out with *"Blessed is the man . . . ."* Then the passage goes on to describe the blessed or successful person. But the chapter starts off with what you might describe as the "negative" side, because verse 1 says, *"Blessed is the man that walketh NOT in the counsel of the ungodly, nor standeth in the way of sinners, nor sitteth in the seat of the scornful."* In other words, this chapter first tells us what the blessed person does *not* do!

Emphasis on the Negative Can Be Positive!

Many Christians want to learn all the positive aspects of success, but not nearly as many want to hear anything that's negative in connection with success. These people are what I call "ostrich Christians." Like the ostrich, they want to bury their heads in the sand, thinking that no one will see them or that all of their problems will just go away. They have the attitude, *If I just make positive confessions and don't ever acknowledge anything negative, I will be a success.*

But sometimes you *have* to look at the negative side of things. Sometimes, to accentuate the positive, you have to look at the negative first so you'll know where you are; what you're supposed to do to improve your situation; and what you are *not* supposed to do! And our text, Psalm 1:1-3, tells us both what we *should* and *shouldn't* do if we want to be successful.

Someone might say, "Just preach the *do's*; don't preach the *don'ts*."

Well, in years past, it seemed so many people were preaching the *don'ts* that many Christians became bound by legalism and a sense of condemnation. But now, in more recent years I think that some Christians have gone overboard in the other direction with the *do's.* As a result, they are doing things they shouldn't be doing.

It's about time we bring the "pendulum" back to the middle where it belongs. (It seems that many Christians are forever having trouble staying "in the middle of the road." In other words, they are either too far over on the *do's* side or too far over on the *don'ts* side. But the real truth lies somewhere down the middle.)

I have been called a balanced preacher by many. Personally, I try to bring balance to certain issues by simply preaching the truth, rightly dividing the Word of God (2 Tim. 2:15). Some people have told me that balance is the hallmark of my teaching and preaching, and I appreciate that.

You see, some people are so natural and carnal that they often cause problems for themselves and others. Then on the other side, some people are so "super-spiritual" that they're "no earthly good," and those kinds of people can cause problems too. In my teaching and preaching, I try to pull people out of the ditches on both sides so they can reach their highest potential in Christ, and we can all accomplish more for the Kingdom of God!

I believe it's important to preach on the *don'ts* once in a while. As we've seen in Psalm 1:1, the Bible has something to say about the *don'ts*. It says, *"Blessed is the man that walketh NOT in the counsel of the ungodly, NOR standeth in the way of sinners, NOR sitteth in the seat of the scornful."* In other words, it's saying that the person who wants to be blessed just doesn't do certain things.

First, he doesn't walk in the counsel of the ungodly. Now what does that mean? That means the blessed man doesn't *abide* in the counsel of the ungodly, and he doesn't live or govern his life by it. He shuns or turns his back on that kind of counsel.

Let's read Psalm 1:1 again to see something else the Lord is saying to us: *"Blessed is the man that WALKETH not in the counsel of the ungodly, nor STANDETH in the way of sinners, nor SITTETH in the seat of the scornful."*

I want you to notice that this verse starts out with the word, "walking," and ends up with the word, "sitting." In other words, the sequence indicates we see an increased intimacy — *walking*, *standing*, and then *sitting* — with the things that are not right.

This verse is warning us, if we begin *walking* with those who are ungodly and begin taking their advice, pretty soon we'll be *standing* in their way of life. We'll accept their code of conduct and adopt their values and philosophies. And if we're not careful, we'll eventually find ourselves *sitting* with the scornful.

Beware of the World's Philosophy

One philosophy of the ungodly is the attitude, *It's all right to do anything you want as long as no one gets hurt.* For example, someone with that kind of mentality will say, "It's all right to have a beer or a glass of wine now and then."

But, no, it's not! That's what sinners do. People of God shun the very *appearance* of evil (1 Thess. 5:22). Yet if a man or woman of God begins to "hang around" the ungodly and walk in their ways, he or she will begin to adopt some of their philosophies. That's how it starts — just by hanging around the ungodly a little bit and walking in their counsel.

More than you may realize, it's so important who your friends are and who you fellowship with. Why? Because if you're fellowshipping with the wrong crowd, you will start accepting their code of conduct. Then the natural or logical sequence is that you'll find yourself taking your seat with them, sitting in the seat of the scornful.

One of the devil's greatest conquests in the Church would be to get as many Christians as he could to sit in the seat of the scornful. To "scorn" means to *reject*, *despise*, *deride*, *disdain,* or to *think of with contempt*. And do you know what? It's not always just *sinners* who are scornful.

For example, you could be very disciplined about resisting obvious temptations to sin. But did you know that it's wrong to be scornful of other believers who may not believe exactly the way you do?

Someone who is being scornful of fellow believers might say, "Look at those people over there shouting and praising God. That's foolish; it's not of God." That person despises hearing others shout and praise God, and, by being critical, he is taking his seat with the scornful.

Some Christians, especially some in the "faith movement" have also gotten themselves in the seat of the scornful and have played right into the devil's hands. These people have the attitude about other Christians, *They don't believe quite like we do; therefore, they're not right.*

I'm talking about the Church! We are not to take our seat with the scornful by criticizing fellow believers because they may not believe exactly the way we do. We are to walk in love and fellowship with others who believe in the Lord Jesus Christ as the eternal Son of God and the one and only true Savior of the world.

Certainly, we're not to have close fellowship with those who don't believe the Bible and who are unsaved. We already saw that the Bible talks about *not* walking with those kinds of people.

Someone asked, "Well, what are we going to do then — become hermits?"

No, that's not the answer at all. Did you realize that's the way the monasteries of old were started? They were started because people wanted to pull away from all the evil in the world.

These people thought that if they secluded themselves behind stone walls and didn't let in any evil influence, they would not be bothered by evil! They thought that their rigorous way of life and their religious services would shield them from everything that wasn't good. But those people failed to realize that the devil is a spirit, and stone walls can't stop him! They failed to realize that as a spirit, the devil likes to sit on people's shoulders and talk to their minds and try to influence them.

Renew Your Mind and Resist The World With the Word

A person could shut himself away in a room somewhere like a hermit and still have bad thoughts. So to become a hermit is not the answer for living a holy, separated, and consecrated life.

The answer is to be in Christ and to let *Him* have full control of your life. How do you do that?

First, you must be born again and become a new creature in Him (2 Cor. 5:17). Then you must renew your mind with the Word.

> **ROMANS 12:1,2**
> **1 I beseech you therefore, brethren, by the mercies of God, that ye present your bodies a living sacrifice, holy, acceptable unto God, which is your reasonable service.**
> **2 And be not conformed to this world: but be ye transformed by THE RENEWING OF YOUR MIND, that ye may prove what is that good, and acceptable, and perfect, will of God.**

Notice what Paul said in verse 1: *"I beseech you . . . by the mercies of God, that ye present your bodies a living sacrifice . . . ."* Many people don't like to hear about making sacrifices. (They also don't want to hear anything about God's judgment, especially in regard to *their* being judged!)

But, friend, the Bible tells us how to live a blessed and victorious life in Christ, and it involves living holy or separate from the world's ways. It involves making sacrifices — doing things our flesh doesn't want to do.

Psalm 1:1-3 and Romans 12:1 and 2 show us both how to live holy and the outcome of living holy before God.

PSALM 1:3
3 . . . he shall be like a tree planted by the rivers of water, that bringeth forth his fruit in his season; his leaf also shall not wither; and whatsoever he doeth shall prosper.

ROMANS 12:2
2 . . . be ye transformed by the renewing of your mind, that ye may prove what is that good, and acceptable, and perfect, will of God.

God shows us the way to be successful in life — through obedience to His Word. But there is also such a thing as exhausting the mercy of God. Once a person exhausts God's mercy toward him, he must face the judgment of God.

In the Old Testament, we see the children of Israel exhausting God's mercy time and time again. Judgment would then come when they refused to cooperate with and obey God. God would even tell them ahead of time what would happen if they didn't straighten up and obey Him. He'd send His prophets to warn them, but often the people still didn't listen. It usually wasn't until they were judged and got into trouble that they would cry out to the Lord. And since He's a merciful God, He would hear their cries and deliver them.

After God would deliver the Israelites, they were all right for a while; they'd serve and obey God, and He would bless them. But then they'd turn around and disobey Him, forgetting His Word. Eventually, God would have to judge them again.

You see, what happened to God's own people also happened to the Egyptian people in the Book of Exodus when God sent Moses to Pharaoh — they were judged. Why? Because they rejected the mercy of God. But the Bible talks about judging *yourself* so that you won't be judged (1 Cor. 11:31).

God Wants His People To Be Blessed!

Thank God, there is such a thing as judging yourself. As I said, some people don't like to hear any preaching about judgment. But I believe it's time somebody preached about it. Thank God for all the great things we have because of the Word of God and His goodness. But many people are totally missing out on the blessings of God because of their disobedience to His Word. They are walking with the world — in the counsel of the ungodly — and they are not judging themselves.

The Word of God says, "There is a way that seems right to man, but if he follows that way, he's going to be judged" (Prov. 14:12; 16:25). But the Bible also says that if a person judges himself ahead of time and straightens up his act, he will not bring God's judgment upon himself (Matt. 7:1; Luke 6:37; 1 Cor. 11:31)!

I'm saying that judgment is as much a part of God's Word as faith, prosperity, healing, and all the other good things we like to hear about!

God *wants* us to be blessed in life. That's why He began Psalm 1:1 by saying, *"BLESSED IS THE MAN that walketh not in the counsel of the ungodly, nor standeth in the way of sinners, nor sitteth in the seat of the scornful."* Blessed is the man that does *what*? That walketh *not* in those ways that will eventually get him into trouble!

Mental Reasoning Can Distract You From The Word And Rob You of God's Blessings

Sitting in the seat of the scornful doesn't just automatically *happen* to a person. It starts when he hangs around and fellowships with the wrong people. Then he finds himself listening to what they have to say, and he begins to reason out their advice in his own mind.

The devil will accommodate you if you begin to reason against God's Word, and he will try to use the avenue of reason against you. You see, the devil is the god of this world (2 Cor. 4:4). You contact the world with your mind and your senses. That's why your mind has to be renewed by the Word of God. Then when you hear the counsel of the ungodly, you'll immediately reject it because it doesn't line up with the Word that you have put into your heart or spirit.

So you see, the answer to living a blessed, separated, and sanctified life that is pleasing to God is not to become a hermit and hide yourself away from the world. No, you just need to be who you are in Christ! You need to know who you are in Christ Jesus — a new creation! Then you need to act upon that truth and reap the benefits of it by continually renewing your mind with the Word and doing those things which are pleasing to God.

We Are *in* the World But Not *of* the World

We know that we are not to walk in the counsel of the ungodly — fellowshipping with them and following their advice and practices. But nowhere in the Bible does it say we are to hide ourselves away and totally shun the world and sinners.

Look at Jesus, for example. Jesus ate with sinners, and when the Pharisees protested, He said, "*. . . They that be whole need not a physician, but they that are sick*" (Matt. 9:12). In other words, Jesus came to save the lost, heal the sick, and deliver the captives. He did not despise the ungodly; He *ministered* to them.

Since Jesus used the word "physician" in Matthew 9:12, let's follow that line of thinking for a minute. Let's look at the example of a physician.

Physicians often work with deadly germs. Even though they wear rubber gloves and other protective clothing or equipment, the minute they leave their work area, they take off their gloves, mask, and so forth, and throw them away in a special container. Then they wash their hands very thoroughly.

Although physicians work around sickness, disease, and germs, they keep a clear mind and maintain a clear line of demarcation between health and illness. They understand that they must work under certain conditions to help their patients, but they still take every precaution to remain healthy and not allow themselves to be contaminated by the germs they could be exposed to.

In much the same way, we as Christians must keep a clear mind and maintain a clear line of demarcation between right and wrong and between righteousness and sin when we are ministering to sinners and winning the lost.

There are many Christians who are trying to run with the devil's crowd; they don't know how to keep that line of demarcation. But you can keep that line clear and your mind steady the same way Jesus did — by realizing and understanding that you are *in* this world but not *of* this world. (We'll talk more about that in Chapter 2.)

I want you to notice that Jesus reached out to sinners and ate with them, but if they didn't start following Him, He didn't follow *them*. He was the Lord Jesus Christ. He came to bring sinners life, and they either came into the fold and received that life, or they rejected it and left Him.

Jesus never rejected people; *they* rejected *Him*. Jesus reached out to people, but it was up to them whether they accepted or rejected Him.

We need to reach out to others, too, but we ought to have better sense than to go with them to certain places. For example, I don't agree with some people's philosophy about how to spread the Gospel. For instance, they think it's all right to go into bars to preach the Gospel to sinners.

Unless it's a supernatural move of God prompting us to go into a bar to give someone the Gospel, we don't belong in bars. We can open ourselves up to harm by doing those kinds of things.

Use the Spiritual Discernment God Has Given You — *And Be Blessed*!

Psalm 1:1 says, *"Blessed is the man that walketh not in the counsel of the ungodly . . . ,"* but I like to say, "Blessed is the man that walketh not in the stupidity of the world"! Psalm 1:2 says, *"But his delight is in the law of the Lord; and in his law doth he meditate day and night."* When you "walk not" in the counsel of the ungodly but delight yourself in the Word of God, meditating upon it continually, you *will* be blessed.

The Lord revealed this same truth to Joshua in Joshua chapter 1.

JOSHUA 1:8
8 This book of the law [God's Word] **shall not depart out of thy mouth; but thou shalt meditate therein day and night, that thou mayest observe to do according to all that is written therein: for THEN THOU SHALT MAKE THY WAY PROSPEROUS, and then THOU SHALT HAVE GOOD SUCCESS.**

The *Amplified* version of Joshua 1:8 says, ". . . For then you shall make your way prosperous, and then you shall *deal wisely* and have good success." This verse is talking about being blessed, happy, and successful *in the everyday affairs of life*! Through meditating and acting upon the Word, you can know how to conduct yourself in every situation and circumstance.

Some people just don't exercise what I call "good common sense" when it comes to the everyday affairs of life. As a result, they aren't enjoying "good success" in certain areas. For example, in the United States, the progress of certain political and social issues is being seriously hurt by the drastic actions of a few people.

I believe Christians can make a statement as to what they believe without doing something drastic or militant. Militancy is never going to settle moral issues. One way things can be changed for the better is in the legislative body of our country. That can happen by our voting and putting the right people in office. (I'm not making a statement for or against a particular political party. How people vote should depend on a candidate's principles, not his political affiliation.)

'Walking Not in the Counsel of the Ungodly' Can Keep You From Being Gullible

Another area of life in which some Christians do not "deal wisely" has to do with missions work. Now don't misunderstand me. I am not against anyone who's doing a real work for the Lord. It's important to support missions. But I *am* against those who try to get money for so-called works they've established in other countries, yet those works either don't exist at all or they are nothing like what they're represented to be.

In other words, some people talk about what big works they have in other countries, but when you go to those countries, often the works aren't half as big as they were described or may even be nonexistent!

Friend, it's time we begin to deal wisely in some of these areas. Jesus said, "Be wise as serpents, and harmless as doves" (Matt. 10:16).

'Walking Not in the Counsel of the Ungodly' Can Help You Recognize False Teaching

We also need to use some sense when it comes to false teaching that doesn't line up with the Word of God. Some Christians can be so smart when it comes to business deals. They are astute when they believe someone is trying to take advantage of them in the natural. Yet when it comes to people trying to deceive them *spiritually*, those Christians will believe almost anything! In other words, someone could just "poke" any doctrine down their mouths, so to speak, and they'd "swallow it" like a baby bird with its mouth wide open!

But the other side of that coin is, a person can become so cynical that he's not sensitive to *anything*, not even to God's Word and His Spirit. There has to be a balance in these things. And you achieve that balance by *walking not* in the counsel of the ungodly and by delighting yourself in God's Word!

We need to realize that we have to keep a clear mind if we're going to keep ourselves from being taken in by some of these things we've talked about. We can't allow our minds to become muddled by walking with the wrong crowd.

As I said, Jesus ministered among sinners, but He never became a part of them. The Bible says Jesus "*. . . did not commit himself unto them, because he knew all men, And needed not that any should testify of man: for he knew what was in man*" (John 2:24,25).

The problem with some people is that they're often not wise enough to keep from being drawn in by the sinner's conversation and lifestyle. They reason, "Oh, but, Preacher, they *said* they were

Christians." But First John 4:1 says, *"Beloved, BELIEVE NOT EVERY SPIRIT, BUT TRY THE SPIRITS whether they are of God: because many false prophets are gone out into the world."*

We are to "try the spirits." We are to exercise a little bit of spiritual discernment and not walk in the counsel of the ungodly. I have seen good Spirit-filled Christians getting "sucked into" wrong doctrine like it was quicksand! In other words, they didn't get sucked in all at once; it happened gradually. They began to walk with certain groups that looked good, sounded good, and so forth. But those groups were preaching doctrine that went against the Bible. (Thank God, some people who are deceived do eventually fight their way out of the quicksand of deception.)

Don't Be Moved By Outward Appearances

You see, just because something looks good on the surface does not mean that it *is* good. For example, I like cherry pie, especially the kind with cross-strips of crust on top, sprinkled with sugar. But I'll tell you what — if I walk down the street and see a piece of cherry pie just lying there on the curb, I'm surely not going to eat it!

You may laugh at that illustration, but there's a valuable truth to it that I want you to see. No matter what something may look like on the surface or at first glance, you have to choose wisely if you want to be successful and blessed in life. You must choose your friends rightly, and you must rightly divide the Word of truth so you can hold fast to sound doctrine.

How can you do that? By *not* doing something — by *not* walking in the counsel of the ungodly, by *not* standing in the way of the sinner, and by *not* sitting in the seat of the scornful!

If you keep yourself from getting tangled up in the counsel of the ungodly to begin with, you will never end up at the place of sitting in the seat of the scornful.

Similarly, the Bible says, *"He that walketh with wise men shall be wise . . ."* (Prov. 13:20). This is what will happen when you walk in the counsel of the *godly* — you will be wise!

I want to get you thinking in line with the Word of God. When the Word says you'll be blessed if you do certain things, then do them! And when the Word says you'll be blessed if you *don't* do certain things, then don't do those things! From Genesis to Revelation, we can see that blessed is the man or woman who does what the Word of God says to do or *not* to do!

Chapter 2
We Are Not of This World!

Blessed is the man that walketh not in the counsel of the ungodly, nor standeth in the way of sinners, nor sitteth in the seat of the scornful.

— Psalm 1:1

They [believers] *are not of the world, even as I* [Jesus] *am not of the world.*

— John 17:16

In the last chapter, I discussed "walking not" in the counsel of the ungodly, and I said that you should choose carefully the friends with whom you closely associate. The company you keep does have much to do with whether or not you will be blessed and prosperous as the Word describes in Psalm 1:1-3.

I want to elaborate on that point in this chapter. I realize that as you work and live in this world, you're going to "rub shoulders" with some of the wrong kinds of people. You have to go to work, but you can go, check in, and work without entering into close fellowship with your co-workers and taking on their characteristics and lifestyles.

Remember, the Bible says, "We are *in* this world, but we are not *of* this world" (John 17:16).

Now don't misunderstand me. I'm not saying you shouldn't even talk to others on your job, because your conversation and lifestyle should be a witness to others. But working on the job with unbelievers is not the same as running with or fellowshipping with them on a personal basis.

People choose their friends from many avenues of life — from the business world, social clubs, cultural and intellectual groups or from sports clubs, leagues, and so forth. In other words, the way people enjoy life is usually similar to the way their friends enjoy life. There is usually a common root or thread between you and your friends.

For instance, if you own your own business, some of your friends are probably business owners too. People have a tendency to socialize within the circles where they operate. For example, a very cultured person probably wouldn't hang around some of us who are cowboys!

The Devil's Trap

This matter of whom you associate with on a regular basis is probably the area in which the devil most cleverly operates to get Christians off track. In other words, the devil seems to use more of his clever devices to get people in the "wrong camp" or with the wrong crowd than he does in any other area.

For example, you might work with some ungodly people who enjoy some of the same things you enjoy. Because they like cultural events, they might say to you, "Let's go out to dinner and then see a play."

Or they may love to play softball, and they'll say to you, "Hey, we've formed a softball team, and we need another player. Why don't you join us?" Their invitations seem innocent enough on the surface. Then the devil will even hop on your shoulder and say, "This is a great ministry opportunity." But if you're not careful, you'll set yourself up to be surrounded on a regular basis with the wrong kinds of people. You'll go out to the ball field, and your co-workers will have a cooler or ice chest full of beer, and they'll be standing around telling off-color jokes.

As a Christian, you know you don't belong in that kind of environment. But if you continue to hang out with that crowd, the next thing you know, they'll start having out-of-town tournaments, and they'll want you to come along.

At first, you might hesitate. But the devil will be right there to try to get you to reason out why you should go. He'll say, "You could be a good witness to them if you go. You might even get them to go to church on Sunday while you're in that town." But most of the time, that just doesn't work. (Those guys are going to the tournament to play softball, not to go to church!) You simply need to be careful how you choose your friends.

When I was growing up, I remember that all the social activities our family (and most of the families in my community) attended revolved around the church. In our family, it wasn't a matter of whether or not we were going to the church ice-cream social; it was just a matter of what time we were going to leave to get there!

Certainly there were kids in the neighborhood who weren't saved, and I talked to them. I didn't ignore them, but I didn't pal around with them either. I hung around with the kids from church.

Fellowship With Those Of Like-Precious Faith

If we are going to maintain a strong Christian witness, then we need to understand that part of staying built up spiritually is to engage in social activities with people who are like-minded. We can go out on evangelistic crusades to preach, or we can participate in one-on-one evangelistic outings, knocking on doors and witnessing on the streets. But we should come back to the flock for our social activities.

If you are continually fellowshipping with the world, it will become very easy for you to gradually get pulled over into the philosophies of the world until you begin thinking as the world thinks. But blessed is the man who doesn't fall into this trap!

Beware of Worldly Trappings And Distractions

I once heard a story about a man who visited a certain town for a business appointment. When he arrived, he discovered that there was a parade going through town, and the street where he needed to turn was blocked. The man saw other people joining the parade, so he said, "That's what I'll do! I'll join the parade, and when I get to my street, I'll just veer off and go to my appointment."

The man joined the parade and got so involved waving at the people and talking back and forth with the onlookers that he missed his street! He got to the end of the parade and missed his appointment entirely!

That's similar to what happens to Christians many times. They try to see how closely involved with the world they can get and still remain in fellowship with God. But they usually end up missing out on God's best. Of course, we should be a witness to a lost and dying world. But we can't be as effective in our witness if we live so close to the world that we blend in with it. When we do that, we lose our effectiveness for God.

You see, the kind of people you run with will be the kind of person you'll become. It has been said that if you run with people who walk like ducks and quack like ducks, it won't be long before people will be calling you a duck!

If a person is an automobile mechanic, you will be able to tell that he works on cars just by looking at his clothes when he comes home from work at the end of the day. Or if a person is a painting contractor, you can tell by looking at him that he paints! Their occupations show up on the outside!

So you see, whatever you are doing and whomever you are running with will show up on the outside. I'm talking about living in line with the Word and staying away from the influence of the world.

Thank God for all the great things we have learned from God's Word about faith and who we are in Christ. But one of the great truths from the Word that many have not learned or have lost to a large extent is holiness and right living before God.

I say that because the only visible difference between the lifestyle of some Christians and the world is that those Christians *call* themselves Christians. But there needs to be a greater consecration and separation than just calling themselves Christians. And the Bible agrees. It says, *"Blessed is the man that walketh not in the counsel of the ungodly, nor standeth in the way of sinners, nor sitteth in the seat of the scornful"* (Ps. 1:1)!

As a Christian, it's very hard to have close contact with the world's crowd and keep your virtue. So what is the answer? The following story I once read might help you and give some guidelines to living the blessed, separated life that Psalm 1 talks about.

Hold On to the Father's Hand

A little girl and her father were walking along the banks of a nice flowing river. The girl was picking flowers and saw a beautiful grass-covered islet that jutted out on the river. She wanted to run ahead of her father to pick some of the flowers that covered this small area of land, but her father stopped her and said, "No. Don't go."

"Why can't I go?" the little girl asked.

The father took his daughter around to another side of the little islet. At that particular angle, the little girl could clearly see that it was not solid ground but only a thin crust of dirt that lay over the water's surface. Had the little girl run onto it, she would have fallen into the swiftly flowing river.

The little girl said to her father, "I would have been in great trouble had I run out there." Then she said, "I'd still like to have some of the flowers there. Is there a way we can get some?"

The father answered, "You can go out as far as you want and pick all the flowers you like — as long as you can still hold on to my hand."

You see, that islet looked beautiful to the little girl, but it wasn't all that it appeared to be. In the same way, we might see something that looks great, but we need to be careful that we don't go along with it just because it looks good. We need to see if something lines up with God's Word before we get involved with it.

The example of that little girl and her father is a good guideline to live by: You can do whatever you want to do — *if* you can do it and still hold on to God's hand! Following that rule will help you draw the line, because you can't hold on to God's hand and still run with certain people. It's just that simple.

So follow that "rule of thumb" — whatever you do in life, make sure you can do it and still hold on to the Father's hand.

It is said that the mother of the great preacher John Wesley made a similar statement. Of course, her statement was recorded in more of an Old English style of writing, but the principle is still the same. She said, "Would you judge the lawfulness or the unlawfulness of pleasure, take this rule: [Avoid] whatever impairs in tenderness your conscience, weakens your reasoning, obscures your sense of God, or takes off the relish of spiritual things."

The phrase "Would you judge" means "If you were going to judge." In other words, she said, "If you were going to judge whether a pleasure was lawful or unlawful, follow this rule . . . ." Then she said, ". . . whatever impairs in tenderness your conscience . . . ." In other words, she was saying that whatever takes away from the tenderness of your conscience, making it hard and insensitive, should be avoided.

She finished by saying, ". . . [whatever] weakens your reasoning, obscures your sense of God, or takes off the relish of spiritual things." She was talking about things that would cause a person to fall away from God and to see spiritual things as less important or sacred.

Someone else said, "Whatever increases the authority of the body over your mind, that thing to you is a sin." That's a pretty strong statement, but it contains a lot of truth.

Did you ever notice that when it comes to the world, everything is geared toward sensuality and the sense realm? For example, every product you see advertised on a billboard or on television — even during the evening news or a sports program — is sold through sensualism. What is presented to your eye gate and your ear gate is designed to appeal to your senses. You have to be careful that you don't get involved with that stuff.

Don't get so caught up in the mental and sensual realms that you lose out in the things of the Spirit. You don't have to conform to the world's way of doing things, because the Bible says, *"BLESSED is the man that walketh NOT in the counsel of the ungodly, nor standeth in the way of sinners, nor sitteth in the seat of the scornful"* (Ps. 1:1)!

Be Wise, Not Worldly

Some Christians will argue, "Yes, but we've got to sell the Gospel." No, we do *not* have to *sell* the Gospel. The Word of God says to *preach* the Gospel (Mark 16:15)! It did *not* say, "Go out and try to *prove* the Gospel." It just said, "Preach it"!

We have to be careful not to get involved with some of the philosophies and studies of the world, even those that are supposed to be spiritual. Not everything that seems spiritual is actually of God. Concerning false doctrine, for example, some message you read or hear taught may *look* good and *seem* good. But it doesn't matter who's teaching it; if it doesn't line up with the Word of God, you shouldn't receive or get involved with it.

The Apostle Paul was very strong on that subject. He said, *"But though we, or an angel from heaven, preach any other gospel unto you than that which we have preached unto you, let him be ACCURSED. As we said before, so say I now again, If any man preach any other gospel unto you than that ye have received, let him be ACCURSED"* (Gal. 1:8,9).

We need to be careful in these days. We need to get so taken up with God and His Word that all of the distractions and trappings of the world can have no place in us. Then we will be able to experience the *continual* flow of God's blessings that He wants us to have. *That's* what it means to have success in life!

Chapter 3
Obedience to the Word Brings Great Blessing!

> *Blessed is the man that walketh not in the counsel of the ungodly, nor standeth in the way of sinners, nor sitteth in the seat of the scornful.*
>
> *BUT HIS DELIGHT IS IN THE LAW OF THE LORD; and in his law doth he meditate day and night.*
>
> *And he shall be like a tree planted by the rivers of water, that bringeth forth his fruit in his season; his leaf also shall not wither; and whatsoever he doeth shall prosper.*
>
> — Psalm 1:1-3

The degree of blessing we receive from God is largely up to us and the decisions we make in life. We can decide to obey God's Word from our heart and be blessed as a result, or we can choose to disobey God's Word and act contrary to what God has said. When we disobey, God's blessing can't rest upon us like He wants it to, because He can't bless disobedience. So, you see, the choice of whether or not we're successful and blessed by God is up to *us*.

There are many blessings of God that are promised to those who obey Him and His Word. In every situation of life, if you will ask yourself *What does the Word say?* and then *act* on the Word in obedience, you will be blessed in your situation or circumstance. But before you can properly obey the Word, you've got to know what it says. You can know the Word by studying and meditating on it. The Word has to be your number-one priority in life if you want to live in the fullness of God's blessings.

Look at verse 2 of our text: *"But his delight is in the law of the Lord . . . ."* Who is this verse talking about? *Whose* delight is in the Law of the Lord?

The answer can be found in verse 1: *the man that walketh not in the counsel of the ungodly*! He has his delight in the Law or in the Word of the Lord.

You see, when you discover what the delight of a person's life is, you will find out what the most important thing is to him or her.

For some people, the delight of their life is something other than the Word of God. But for us as believers, that should not be.

You can often tell what a person's delight is just by talking to him. For instance, you could mention a certain subject, and he might light up like a light bulb in a dark room. You have just discovered what his delight is.

You Can Determine Your Own Destiny!

You'll also find that wherever your delight is, that is where all your energies are directed. I once read the following example that illustrates this truth, and I want to share it with you:

Two young men of the same age and from the same small town each moved to the big city. One of them immediately sought out the university and all that it could offer him. He also sought out a place where he could attend church.

The other young man was attracted to the night life — the "hot spots," the clubs, the taverns, and the music. It's pretty easy to predict the outcome of each of these young men because of where they each placed their delight and attention. One of them focused on furthering his education and making something of himself. The other young man slept all day and caroused all night.

The choice whether or not to delight yourself in the Law of the Lord will determine your destiny!

The Law of the Lord Provides Light To Walk In

What does the Law of the Lord do? Well, for one, it tells you what is right or wrong. It also shows you all the possibilities that exist for you because of what Jesus did for you in His death, burial, and resurrection.

But there's another thing that the Law of the Lord does that many people don't like: It shows them the right way and the wrong way to go and the consequences of both ways. People get excited about the possibilities that exist for them in Christ, but some don't want to do the things that *put them in position* to receive God's best for their lives. They don't want to go the right way in life; instead, they want to go the wrong way.

You see, in the Law of the Lord, not only can you determine your destiny or outcome in life — you can also find out how to *change* your destiny or the path you're currently on.

What do I mean by that? Your decision to delight yourself in the Law of the Lord can cause you to walk in victory instead of defeat. The Bible holds certain promises for those who will seek God and accept His Word as absolute truth.

We talk about the fact that we have been redeemed from the curse of the Law through the blood of the Lord Jesus Christ. But God doesn't just want us to *know* that; He wants us to actually walk in and *experience* the blessings of our redemption — freedom from poverty, sickness, and spiritual death!

Another thing that the Law of the Lord shows us is our duties as children of God. For example, natural Israel was known as the children of God in the Old Testament. They were God's people (Exod. 3:7-10; 1 Kings 8:16).

Well, have you ever read in the Old Testament that the children of Israel had responsibilities given to them by God! In other words, He said, "If you do such-and-such, I will do such-and-such."

DEUTERONOMY 11:26-28
26 Behold, I set before you this day a blessing and a curse;
27 A blessing, if ye obey the commandments of the Lord your God, which I command you this day:
28 And a curse, if ye will not obey the commandments of the Lord your God, but turn aside out of the way which I command you this day, to go after other gods, which ye have not known.

We, too, have become God's people through the blood of the Lord Jesus Christ. And over in the New Testament, we find out that the *spiritual* children of God have many responsibilities too. For example, Mark 11:24 says, ". . . *What things soever ye desire, when ye pray, believe that ye receive them, and* [then] *ye shall have them.*"

You see, one of our responsibilities is to pray and to believe that we receive. No matter how badly God may want to bless us and give us something, He can't unless we've done our part: believe we receive when we pray. And when our part is fulfilled, God will do His part: He will make sure that we have whatever it is we were believing for!

JOHN 16:23,24,26
23 And in that day ye shall ask me nothing. Verily, verily, I say unto you, Whatsoever ye shall ASK the Father in my name, he will give it you.
24 Hitherto have ye asked nothing in my name: ASK, and ye shall receive, that your joy may be full . . . .
26 At that day ye shall ASK in my name . . . .

I want you to notice that in those verses, Jesus kept saying, "Ask. Ask. *Ask* that you might receive! *Ask* that your joy might be full!" The Father knows our needs, but Jesus said for us to ask Him for whatever it is we want or need. So you see, we have responsibilities. And one of them is to *ask*.

The Bible also says, *"Not forsaking the assembling of ourselves together, as the manner of some is; but exhorting one another: and so much the more, as ye see the day approaching"* (Heb. 10:25). That's another responsibility — not forsaking the assembling of ourselves together!

We have a responsibility to be committed to a local body of believers — to a local church. Yes, there is the universal Church, but we also have local bodies all over the world. And we are to come together in those local bodies and meet on a regular basis.

The Early Church met together regularly (Acts 2:46). The members of each of the churches Paul established in his missionary journeys met together also (Acts 20:7; 1 Cor. 15:4). Why did they meet together? To worship God and to find out about the things of God so that they could walk in more light and receive more of what God said belonged to them.

God's Blessings Are Conditional

As I said before, some people don't want to hear about the fact that they have some responsibilities according to the Word and that *they* are going to have to do something to receive them. As long as they can jump, shout, kick up their heels, and holler "Glory, hallelujah" about something, then they are all in favor of God's blessings. But when the preacher starts talking about Christian duty, that's more than they bargained for, and they're not too happy about that!

But the Bible itself talks about what God requires of us — it's not just some idea I or some other preacher dreamed up! The Bible talks plainly about the Christian's responsibility.

Someone may say, "I didn't think we were supposed to work for our salvation." No, of course we're not to work for our salvation. We're to believe *God* for our salvation (Eph. 2:8,9). We are saved by grace through faith; we don't perform works in order to be saved. But after we are saved, we are supposed to work for God — not to earn anything, but just because we love Him and we *want* to serve Him because of all He's done for us.

The Apostle Paul talked about the fact that he was in debt to God. In other words, Paul was serving God because of what God had done for him. It was a love relationship of service, not a relationship based on fear and bondage (Rom. 1:1).

It's sort of like the servants in the Bible who were able to go free after a certain time, but because they loved their masters so much, they chose to stay and serve them (*see* Deut. 15:12-17). Similarly, we're free to go our own way and "do our own thing" in life, but because we love God — because of what He's done for us — we choose to serve Him. We choose to take on the responsibilities outlined in the Word. When we do that and begin to believe God for what He says belongs to us, He blesses us more and more. We serve Him because of His goodness to us, and the blessings just keep coming!

Actually, the Bible says, "These blessings shall *overtake* you" (Deut. 28:2). When you're busy working for God and being obedient to what He says, you don't always have to believe for the blessings. They will just come your way and overtake you because you're fulfilling your responsibilities.

Certainly, we're to pray and believe God for things the Bible tells us we can have, but when we're willing and obedient, we can rest assured that we will eat the good of the land (Isa. 1:19)!

To Love God Is To Live in Line With His Word

You can't be willing and obedient to God in everything if you're not delighting yourself in the Law of the Lord.

PSALM 1:2
2 But his delight is in the law of the Lord; and in his law doth he meditate day and night.

The blessed man's delight is in the Law of the Lord, and in that Law doth he meditate, *how much*? *Some* of the time? No. *Day* and *night*. In other words, he meditates on God's Word all the time. Seven days a week, twenty-four hours a day, and sixty minutes an hour, he thinks about the Word of God and the things of God.

You see, when you are familiar with the Law of the Lord, your thinking changes. When you think about God's Law — His Word — you are thinking about God's plan, because His *Word* and His *will* are one. Then when you do what the Word says, the Word becomes such a part of you that your judgment and your decisions are not based on anything but the Law of the Lord.

You can become so saturated with what the Bible says that when you face a crisis or an important decision, your judgment will not be based on the world or the counsel of the ungodly. Your decisions will be based upon the Word of God. For example, in the time of financial crisis, your decisions will not be based on what the economists are saying but on what *God* is saying! In the time of a physical crisis or challenge, your decisions will not be based on what the doctors say but on what God says. Why? Because your delight is in the Law of the Lord, and the Word of God is the most precious thing in the world to you.

Somebody asked me one time, "If someone had the power to take from you every material thing you have — your bank account, your house, your car, your clothes — but said you could keep one thing, what would that one thing be?

I said, "I'd want my Bible."

"Why would you want the Bible?"

I answered, "Because if I have God's Word, I can replace everything that was taken from me. But if I lose God's Word, I don't really have anything anyway."

How To Really Stand Out in a Crowd!

Up to this point, we've been dealing with the "negative" side of Psalm 1, talking about what *not* to do in order to be blessed. But, as I said, sometimes you have to talk about the negative side of things in order to really benefit from the positive.

Now I want to go to the "positive" side of this passage of Scripture and look at some *results* of delighting in the Law of the Lord.

PSALM 1:3
3 And he shall be like a tree planted by the rivers of water, that bringeth forth his fruit in his season; his leaf also shall not wither; and whatsoever he doeth shall prosper.

The man who delights himself in the Law of the Lord shall be like a tree planted by the water.

Have you ever been across a desert or a wide-open plain? There's plenty of wide-open flatland in western Oklahoma and parts of Kansas, Texas, New Mexico, and Arizona. As you're driving across those areas within the states, every once in a while, you can see a group of trees. Although the area looks like a desert plain, when you see trees, you can be assured that there's water out there somewhere! If you drive near those trees, you may find that they're situated on a small river or stream bank. For miles, everything else around those trees might be nothing but dried-up sage brush and prickly mesquite bushes. But those trees are green and beautiful.

That's what the psalmist is talking about in Psalm 1:3: *"And he shall be like a tree planted by the rivers of water, that bringeth forth his fruit in his season; his leaf also shall not wither; and whatsoever he doeth shall prosper."*

When you delight in the Law of the Lord, it doesn't matter what kind of desert situation the devil tries to put you in, you're going to flourish.

And just as a green tree stands out in the natural when everything around it is scrub-brush brown, everyone will see that you're flourishing in the midst of *your* desert!

Notice something else in Psalm 1:3 about the person who is like the tree planted by the rivers of water: He *". . . bringeth forth his fruit IN HIS SEASON . . . ."*

What does that mean? Well, there are a lot of people believing God for something, but they want it "yesterday." They may be trying to believe God for things they don't have enough faith to receive just yet. They may know the faith principles, but they may not know how to apply them properly or how to *keep* them applied over a period of time. So they're not receiving anything.

What they need to do is continually delight themselves in the Law or the Word of God. Then over a period of time, they'll have their root system established. They will know how to draw their strength from the Lord and stand their ground in the hard places when the tests, trials, and storms of life assail them.

Then I want you to notice what that person will become: *". . . he shall be like a tree planted by the rivers of water, that bringeth forth his fruit in his season; HIS LEAF ALSO SHALL NOT WITHER; and whatsoever he doeth shall prosper."*

His leaf will not wither — that means it's not going to dry up! You see, when a tree is planted by a river, the roots of the tree go deep into the ground and eventually spread underneath the river channel. The bigger the tree's root system, the more nourishment that tree receives and the more immovable it becomes.

Sin Can Have No Place in You If You Are Delighting in the Word

A person will not dry up spiritually if his "roots" are spread deep down into the Word of God. There's all kinds of nourishment in the Word of God, and the spiritual man who is rooted in the Word will not dry up. He will not allow strife, envy, bitterness, and other attitudes to come into him. Those kinds of attitudes will cause his leaves to wither.

"Well," you may say, "I just don't know whether I can forgive that person or not." If that is your attitude, you'd better check up on your root system, because your tap root is probably just about severed! If you don't correct that kind of attitude, you'll gradually notice that good things are not happening in your life as they should be or as they did before you allowed unforgiveness and bitterness to take root in your life.

You cannot have unforgiveness in your heart against anyone and still expect to have a healthy root system that's established deep in the Word of God. It doesn't matter what someone has done to you, you can't be bitter or hold a grudge and still expect to receive from God. That means you can't hold anything against *yourself* either!

There are many people who can't forgive themselves. Yes, there is such a thing as forgiving one's self! Certainly, you may have missed it and made a mistake. But if you've confessed your sin and asked God to forgive you, He has forgiven you. So you need to forgive *yourself*.

Then notice another blessing of the person who continually delights himself in the Lord: "*. . . whatsoever he doeth shall prosper*" (Ps. 1:3).

Delighting in the Word Means Doing the Word

Notice that verse said, "*. . . whatsoever he DOETH shall prosper.*" There are many people who are just sitting around *claiming* when they should be out *doing*. They may think they qualify for certain blessings simply because they don't walk in the counsel of the ungodly. And they may even say they are delighting themselves in the Law of God. However, they aren't *cooperating* with God and His Word — because He said He'd bless what they put their hand to, but they're not putting their hand to anything!

For example, I've heard people say, "I believe God is leading me to go into a certain kind of business."

I'd say, "Fine. What are you doing about what He's leading you to do."

"Oh, nothing," they'd answer. "I'm just claiming it and waiting for God to make it happen."

"He won't," I'd say. "He's the One who's bringing the ideas to you and trying to urge you to go out and check on certain things. But you're the one who will have to go out and do something!"

(Now some people will take what I just said and run off with it into the ditch, so to speak, and allow the devil to use it against them. For example, they'll be working a certain job and say, "Well, I feel like I need a change. *Maybe* God is leading me to quit." So they jump too soon to make the change, and things get messed up.)

I'm talking about cooperating with God's leading and operating in line with His Word so He can bless you. When you know that God is leading you a certain way, you've got to take the first step. He can guide your steps, but He can't *guide* your steps if you aren't *taking* any steps!

I was talking to Dad one time years ago about a particular situation in my life. He asked me, "Well, what are you doing about it?"

I said, "I'm believing God."

"That's not enough," he answered.

I said, "What do you mean, 'That's not enough'? That's what you preach."

He said, "You're like a lot of people who sit in my meetings and only get half of what I'm saying." Then he proceeded to quote me a scripture from James: "*. . . shew me thy faith without thy works, and I will shew thee my faith by my works*" (James 2:18).

In other words, my dad was saying, "*You've* got to do something, and believe God while you're doing it. Then the Bible says that what you *do* will prosper."

Well, that was scriptural advice. Psalm 1:3 says, "*And he shall be like a tree planted by the rivers of water, that bringeth forth his fruit in his season; his leaf also shall not wither; and whatsoever he DOETH shall prosper.*"

Years ago, a man in my congregation came up to me and said, "You know, Pastor, I feel like the Lord has given me an idea to go into a certain business."

I said, "Well, if you believe the Lord gave you the idea, then go ahead and believe Him and do it!"

He did, and it has worked all these years. The man has his own successful business.

Now what if that man would have just continued to sit around, saying, "I really believe God has given me this idea. I believe He wants to do something with it, but I'm just waiting on Him, believing Him to cause it to happen." The man would have still been sitting there without any business!

But he didn't just sit there. He went out and went to work with his faith, and now he's enjoying the fruits of putting action to his faith.

There is another aspect that Psalm 1:3 applies to and that's the area of volunteering in the church. I often hear people in our church say, "I want to get involved. I believe God wants me to volunteer in some capacity in the church." Then from the pulpit, the pastoral staff and I will make announcement after announcement about needing help in certain areas. And some of the same people who said they wanted to get involved just sit there, saying, "Well, I'm believing God to show me what to do."

Friend, you could say you're believing God until you fell over, but you'll never get a place in the ministry until you learn to start putting your hand to something! You may feel as though God wants you in a public ministry, but you may have to work in the parking lot or clean the church rest rooms awhile first!

Some people who want a pulpit ministry will say, "Oh, no. I don't want to do *that*. I don't want to clean the church; I want to get on the platform and preach and teach." But it just doesn't work that way.

You've got to be faithful where you're at if you want to be promoted in ministry. For example, I know for myself that before I ever preached to many people, I mowed many church yards, hammered many nails, built many Sunday school rooms, and repaired many roofs.

I've driven thousands of miles, unloaded boxes, and set up sound systems for meetings so someone else could preach and teach. In other words, I did a whole lot of things that had nothing to do with preaching, but they had a lot to do with my being in the position that I am in today!

I said all that to illustrate to you that you've got to be faithful where you are at if you want to be promoted in the ministry. And while you're being faithful, you've got to delight yourself in the Law of the Lord. *Then* whatever you put your hand to in faith, God will prosper.

Delighting in God's Word Makes a Person *Balanced*

To delight yourself in the Law of the Lord means to come in line with the Word of God in every area of life, not just in spiritual matters. As I said before, some people are so "heavenly" minded that they're no earthly good. One pastor once asked me, "Do you have any problems with spiritual 'weirdos' in your church?"

I said, "Not a whole lot."

He said, "What do you attribute that to?"

I said, "Number one, I have people in my church who delight themselves in the Word, and they know what's what. They will squelch a lot of the nonsense that others may try to stir up.

"Number two," I explained, "some of these super-spiritual kinds of people won't mess around in a church if they see a strong spiritual figure providing the right kind of leadership."

I told this pastor, "The first thing you need to do is to teach your church the Word. The second thing you need to do is to provide strong leadership."

I have taught my own local congregation about the gifts of the Spirit so that if someone gets up and starts doing something that's not of God, they just won't go along with it!

"Yes," somebody said, "but it might be the Holy Spirit they're ignoring."

Well, if a person gets into the Word and delights himself in the Law of the Lord, he will know it when God starts moving! No one will have to tell him.

That's just one reason to delight yourself in the Law of the Lord and apply the Word to every area of your life — so you won't be so heavenly minded that you're no earthly good.

Another reason for delighting in the Word and coming in line with it in every area of life has to do with having a successful home and family life.

For example, I have heard parents who said they wanted their children involved in the church. But then, when these same parents had to get out of bed to go pick the children up from a late-night skating party sponsored by the church, they griped and complained about having to do it.

But let me tell you something. It would be much better for those parents to get up and go pick up their children from a church skating party than to have to go to the police station to get their children because they'd gotten into trouble!

When my kids were growing up, many times my flesh didn't want to participate in some of the young people's activities of the church, but I got involved anyway. I made sure my kids were at those activities. Many times, I had to get out of bed in the early hours of the morning to go pick them up at the church. Sometimes I even went on their outings and events to assist in any way I could. No, I didn't necessarily *want* to, but I got involved because I wanted my kids to grow up delighting themselves in the Law of the Lord because they saw me set the right example according to the Word (Gen. 18:19; Eph. 6:4). I wanted my kids to grow up and become involved with the activities of their own children one day.

So you see, God will prosper you if you delight yourself in the Law of the Lord. Why? Because when you truly delight yourself in God's Word, you will begin to act in line with the Word, and that gives God something to work with. Whatever you put your hand to, He will prosper!

Say this out loud: "Every hour, every day, and every night, I think about God and the things of God. Because I meditate in the Law of the Lord, I observe to do it. Therefore, I make my way prosperous and have good success [Joshua 1:8]. And I shall be like a tree planted by the rivers of water that will bring forth fruit in its season. My leaf also shall not wither, and whatever I do will prosper!"

Chapter 4
Renew Your Mind And Become a Success!

This book of the law shall not depart out of thy mouth; but thou shalt MEDITATE therein day and night, that thou mayest observe to do according to all that is written therein: for then thou shalt make thy way prosperous, and then thou shalt have good success.

— Joshua 1:8

The Bible has a lot to say about the mind. In our text, the word "meditate" implies that you are to use your mind to think and dwell upon the Word of God. Why is it so important to think about the Word? Because God's Word is His will, and when we are thinking in line with the Word, we are thinking in line with God's thoughts!

We need to have God's thoughts uppermost in our minds at all times, because our own natural thoughts are small and weak compared to God's thoughts.

ISAIAH 55:8,9
8 For my thoughts are not your thoughts, neither are your ways my ways, saith the Lord.

9 For as the heavens are higher than the earth, SO ARE MY WAYS HIGHER THAN YOUR WAYS, AND MY THOUGHTS THAN YOUR THOUGHTS.

You see, our natural thoughts are limited to what we have learned in life and to our experiences. Our natural thoughts are limited to our environment and can hold us in bondage by confusing us and producing fear and failure in our lives. For example, our thoughts can keep us in constant fear of the future, because our knowledge is limited; we don't know what the future holds.

But God knows the future — He's already been there! And He holds our future in His hands if we will submit to Him and His Word and learn to think in line with His thoughts. God's thoughts are infinitely intelligent and wise. God's thoughts produce liberty and abundant life. That's why the Apostle Paul commanded us to renew our mind with the Word of God.

ROMANS 12:2
2 . . . be not conformed to this world: but be ye transformed by the renewing of your mind, that ye may prove what is that good, and acceptable, and perfect, will of God.

Romans 12:2 is saying basically the same thing that Joshua 1:8 says: God wants us to do something with our minds! He wants us to meditate upon *His* thoughts until our thinking is changed or renewed and we begin to think like He thinks! Then we will be "transformed" and have the good success that the Word of God talks about.

When your mind is renewed with the Word of God, others around you may be filled with fear and uncertainty about the future, but you are at peace. You are thinking God's thoughts, and the promises of God have become rooted and established in your heart. You know that your future is secure because you're trusting God, and you know He will never let you down!

Friend, if you are in Christ, there is really no need for you to have any fear! Looking at the children of Israel in the Old Testament who eventually went in and possessed the Promised Land, you can see that as long as they stayed with God, they were all right. In other words, as long as they believed and obeyed His Word and kept His thoughts in their minds, they were blessed and protected (Josh. 1:13-18). They didn't listen to their natural thoughts that undoubtedly told them, *You will never make it into the Promised Land. Did you see the giants living in that land? You could never accomplish such a feat!*

Today when someone has a God-given vision to accomplish something for the Lord, there are always people who will respond, "That's impossible; you can't do that!" They say that because their minds haven't been renewed with the Word of God, and their thoughts are dominated by failure.

Sometimes, when someone has a strong vision of something God has given him to do, others will say something like, "You must be out of your mind!"

Have you ever heard that expression? Well, we read in Isaiah 55:8 that God's thoughts are not our thoughts; neither are His ways our ways. So to the natural mind — to the person whose mind isn't renewed with the Word — the things of God do not always make sense (1 Cor. 2:14). But if I had a choice between *obeying and being blessed by God* and *making sense to everyone around me*, I'd rather obey God and be "out of my mind"!

'Lose Your Mind' And Become a Success!

Sometimes you have to "lose your mind" to become a success in God!

Before you misunderstand, let me explain what I mean by that statement. You see, in order to obtain the blessings that the Word promises, you have to receive them by faith. That means you have to believe what God says in spite of natural circumstances that may be saying something else.

Well, we know that we believe with our heart or spirit, not our mind. Our mind may be telling us we're not going to receive the answer this time. But we have to "lose" our natural way of thinking and refuse to give place to negative thoughts of doubt or unbelief. We have to stand our ground and give place to our spirit, believing and confessing God's Word until we see the answer. Then we will begin to walk in the success that God has designed for us.

As I mentioned, the things of God are foolishness to the natural mind. Those who walk only according to their natural thinking cannot please God, because the Bible says that without *faith*, it is impossible to please Him (Heb. 11:6). And we already saw that God's thoughts and ways are higher than our ways.

For example, the world has the idea that the only way to the top in life is to climb the ladder of success, so to speak, and step on whomever gets in the way. But the Bible says that to be the greatest, you must be the servant of all (Mark 9:35; 10:44).

Philippians 2:5-11 is another New Testament passage that tells what kind of mind or attitude we are to have.

PHILIPPIANS 2:5-11
5 LET THIS MIND BE IN YOU, which was also in Christ Jesus:
6 Who, being in the form of God, thought it not robbery to be equal with God:
7 But made himself of no reputation, and took upon him the form of a servant, and was made in the likeness of men:
8 And being found in fashion as a man, he humbled himself, and became obedient unto death, even the death of the cross.

> **9 WHEREFORE GOD ALSO HATH HIGHLY EXALTED HIM, and given him a name which is above every name:**
> **10 That at the name of Jesus every knee should bow, of things in heaven, and things in earth, and things under the earth;**
> **11 And that every tongue should confess that Jesus Christ is Lord, to the glory of God the Father.**

Jesus submitted Himself to the will of the Father and obeyed Him even unto "the death of the Cross" (v. 8). And verse 9 says that God highly exalted Him as a result of His obedience.

So many times we as Christians aren't blessed by God as we should be, and we live below our rights and privileges in Christ. Why? Because we haven't submitted ourselves to the will of the Father as Jesus did. We haven't submitted ourselves to His Word by renewing our minds with the Word of God. In other words, we haven't "lost our minds" to become a success in God. We haven't "lost" or put aside our natural way of thinking so we can walk by faith in God's Word instead of walking by sight.

To be a success in God, we have to lose our own way of thinking and take on the mind of Christ.

You may find it hard to believe, but some people will actually read in the Word what God has to say about certain things — what His will is — and then make a remark such as: "*I* think *I* would have handled the situation differently" or "*I* think God should have done it *this* way"!

Friend, that's not submitting to the Word and the will of the Father.

For illustrations, I frequently refer to my military training in the U. S. Army. As a new enlistee, as soon as you arrive at boot camp, you learn right away that what *you* think — your opinion — is unimportant as far as the military is concerned. In fact, when you go into the Army, the first thing they tell you is, "*You* don't think; *we* will think *for* you!"

I'm not trying to compare God with the military. I'm just trying to make the point that when it comes to what the Word of God has to say about a certain situation, what we think about it becomes unimportant in the light of what *God* thinks.

It would be great if every time someone became born again, we could simply tell him, "Now quit leaning to your own understanding or way of thinking and let the mind of Christ be in you" (Prov. 3:5; Phil. 2:5).

However, renewing your mind and having the mind of Christ is an ongoing practice; it takes time and effort. But the rewards are tremendous! When we learn to have the mind of Christ, things can change in our lives for the better. We can stop living beneath our privileges in Christ. Certainly, when we're born again, we still live in the natural world. But we don't have to think just in the natural. We can begin thinking *super*naturally!

Be a 'Supernatural' Thinker!

There are many Christians who are "natural" thinkers. In other words, they lean to their own understanding instead of to God's Word. They think according to how they feel and what they see — according to natural circumstances — instead of thinking in line with the Word. They believe what the news media and economists say *over* what *God* says.

But God wants us to be *super*natural thinkers! He wants us to "lose our minds," so to speak, and become successful in Him!

I believe that when you "lose your mind" concerning your old, natural way of thinking, you also lose any attitude problems you might have. You get God's attitude instead — the attitude of love! And when you renew your mind and begin to think in line with God's Word and His thoughts, you begin to think big! Why? Because God is a big God; He does not think small or "second best."

For example, in the Old Testament when the Israelites were instructed to build a tabernacle in the wilderness, they did it *God's* way — according to *His* thoughts. They could have just cut down a few old blackjack trees or scrub oaks and made poles out of them. Then they could have skinned a few cattle and used the skins to form a shabby covering over the poles. But they didn't do that.

No, God had told them, "Go out and get the best wood. Then cover it with gold and silver" (Exod. 26:32). Then when God gave the instructions for making the priests' robes, He didn't say, "See if you can find someone to sew a couple of pieces of an old flour sack together, and use that for the priestly robe." No, the priests of God were clean, neat, and exquisitely adorned. I mean, those priests had fine gold on their robes with precious stones to trim them (*see* Exodus 39:13).

But today, some Christians think "small" when it comes to the blessings of God. For example, when some people need a new car, they immediately think "*used* car." When some people think about buying a home, they automatically think about buying someone else's home. They never even imagine building a brand-new one. There isn't anything wrong with buying a good secondhand car or home. But when that is *always* the first thought, then they are thinking second-best.

That's why we need to train ourselves with the Word of God and start thinking "success"! But the only way to begin thinking differently is to begin thinking in line with the Word. That's important, because you can't have faith beyond actual knowledge. And we know the Bible says, *"So then faith cometh by hearing, and hearing by the word of God"* (Rom. 10:17).

Think, Speak, and *Act!*

Look again at what the Lord said to Joshua in the Book of Joshua chapter 1.

> **JOSHUA 1:8**
> **8 This book of the law shall not depart out of thy MOUTH; but thou shalt MEDITATE therein day and night, that thou mayest observe to DO according to all that is written therein: for then thou shalt make thy way prosperous, and then thou shalt have good success.**

He said, *"This book of the law shall not depart out of thy mouth . . . ."* Without doing any harm to the Scriptures, we could change that to read, "*The Word of God* shall not depart out of thy mouth." What is the Lord saying? He is saying, "*Speak* the Word!" According to this verse, we are to *think upon*, *speak*, and *act on* the Word!

When you obey this verse of Scripture by thinking upon, speaking, and acting on the Word, you will get the results of this scripture: You'll start having success! Why? Because God said you would!

Furthermore, the truth in these instructions that God gave Joshua worked for Joshua under the Old Covenant (and we know they did, because Joshua and the children of Israel entered in to possess the

Promised Land). Therefore, *how much more* will it work for us under the New Covenant!

Hebrews 8:6 says that we have a better covenant established upon better promises. In other words, the New Covenant entails all that was in the Old Covenant plus *more*! But the first step to obtaining those better promises is to think in line with the Word of God. In order to be blessed as God wants us to be, we must "lose" our own thoughts of unbelief, take hold of the mind of Christ, and think the thoughts of God.

How do you take hold of the mind of Christ and think God's thoughts? By thinking in every situation of life, *What does God think about this situation? What does the Word say about it?*

Having that attitude will change how you think, talk, and act. Thinking upon God's Word will keep you ever aware of His Presence.

There are no shortcuts to having the God-kind of success that Joshua 1:8 talks about. The God-kind of success comes through careful meditation in the Word and renewing your mind with the Word of God. Some people don't like changing the way they think and feel about things. As my father always says, "Their minds are like cement — thoroughly mixed and well set!"

But when it comes to what God has to say about a situation, if our thoughts do not line up with His thoughts, then *we need to change our thoughts!*

Every person's mind contains a conglomeration of ideas, opinions, traditions, and philosophies based upon his or her past experiences, whether good or bad. It's no wonder some people can't think straight! It's no wonder that some people continually live in fear and think in terms of defeat and failure.

They need to "lose" that way of thinking and take hold of God's way of thinking by meditating on the Word of God. Then as the Word takes hold in their heart and mind, it roots out the natural way of thinking that is defeating them.

By way of illustration, there are certain types of grass seed you can plant that take root in the soil and will eventually take over all the other kinds of grass that are growing there. In the same way, we need to "plant" the Word of God into our hearts and minds and let it begin to root out philosophies, opinions, traditions, and ideas that have held us in bondage.

Now do you see what I mean by the statement, "Lose your mind and become a success"?

Man's Way Versus God's Way

I want you to notice again the contrast between the natural way of thinking and God's way of the thinking.

ISAIAH 55:8
8 . . . my thoughts are not your thoughts, neither are your ways my ways, saith the Lord.

Have you ever noticed that many times when God speaks to you and tells you to do something, what He tells you to do is contrary to man's natural way of doing that particular thing? In other words, what God tells you is often contrary to natural thinking.

The Lord said in Luke 6:38, *"Give, and it shall be given unto you; good measure, pressed down, and shaken together, and running over, shall men give into your bosom. For with the same measure that ye mete withal it shall be measured to you again."*

According to God's Word or His way of thinking, if you give, you can expect a benefit or dividend from your giving. But that is contrary to the natural way of thinking.

For example, if someone deposited or invested some of his money in a certain company, he would expect that company to send him a dividend check after a certain period of time. But God says, "Give freely, and *I* will give back to you good measure, pressed down, shaken together, and running over."

People who think only according to the natural believe that if they give money away, they will have less money; so they tend not to give. But according to God's way of thinking, if they give in faith, He will cause it to be given back to them and more besides! But He can't give *back* to a person if he or she hasn't given something in the first place.

God also said in His Word, *"Bring ye all the tithes into the storehouse, that there may be meat in mine house, and prove me now herewith, saith the Lord of hosts, if I will not open you the windows of heaven, and pour you out a blessing, that there shall not be room enough to receive it"* (Mal. 3:10).

That kind of thinking is contrary to the natural laws of economy! Nevertheless, it's God's way of thinking, so we need to come in line with it if we want to be blessed!

The Bible says that the natural man doesn't understand the things of God or His Spirit (1 Cor. 2:14). To the natural man, the Word of God or the things of the Spirit are foolishness. For example, the natural man might hear someone say, "All of my needs are met according to God's riches in glory by Christ Jesus" (Phil. 4:19). The natural man will think the person making that confession is out of his mind! But, no, the person who made that heartfelt confession is on the right track to victory and prosperity in his life!

When it comes to healing, the natural man doesn't understand when someone asks how you're feeling, and *you* say, "I thank God that His Word says I'm healed; by Jesus' stripes, I'm healed!"

Why doesn't the natural man understand that? Because God's thoughts are higher than his thoughts.

Now go on reading that passage in Isaiah 55.

ISAIAH 55:9
9 For as the heavens are higher than the earth, so are my ways higher than your ways, and my thoughts than your thoughts.

To paraphrase that scripture in modern language, we could say, "God's ways are so much higher than ours that we can't comprehend His thoughts with our natural minds."

But to walk in the light of God's Word doesn't require that we fully comprehend God's Word or His way of thinking. However, it does require that we *believe* it. That's where faith comes in, because when you begin thinking thoughts that are so far above your own, you may not have any idea or comprehension how God's Word is going to work in your situation. You just simply have to have faith!

Say this out loud: "The Bible says it, I believe it, and that settles it." You don't necessarily have to understand it, but you do have to firmly believe it!

Have you ever been standing on the Word, thinking God's thoughts and speaking and acting on His Word, and someone said to you, "Could you please explain to me what you're doing"?

Sometimes there is no natural explanation for standing on God's Word despite what circumstances are saying to the contrary. There is only a supernatural explanation, and it is this: "Because God said it, I believe it, and that settles it!"

I believe that's why some people write books against those who teach faith in God's Word — because those people think in the natural, not the supernatural. The idea of believing something a person can't see is foolishness to them. They are limited to believing only in line with what they can understand with their minds.

You see, no matter how great our capacity to reason and analyze, that capacity is nothing compared to the thoughts of God! That's why we sometimes have to explain our believing by saying, "I can't explain it, but I believe it because the Bible says it, and I know it's real."

You Must Believe In Order to Receive

For example, some people ask, "Would you please explain that Holy Ghost business and that business of talking in tongues?" Well, you could explain it to them according to the Word, but they will have to believe it in order to qualify to receive the Holy Ghost for themselves. Some people say, "Well, I just don't believe that whole business about being baptized in the Holy Ghost." Well, that's where their problem lies; they don't believe. And, as I said, you've got to believe God's thoughts, whether you understand them or not, in order to walk in the light of them and receive the blessings of God.

You see, it all comes back to the Word of God. God's Word is God's will. Believing God's Word is the same as believing His thoughts and coming in line with those thoughts.

Look at what else the Bible has to say about God's Word.

ISAIAH 55:10,11
10 For as the rain cometh down, and the snow from heaven, and returneth not thither, but watereth the earth, and maketh it bring forth and bud, that it may give seed to the sower, and bread to the eater:
11 So shall my word be that goeth forth out of my mouth: it shall not return unto me void, but it shall accomplish that which I please, and IT SHALL PROSPER IN THE THING WHERETO I SENT IT.

PSALM 107:20
20 He sent HIS WORD, and HEALED them, and DELIVERED them from their destructions.

According to Isaiah 55:11 and Psalm 107:20, God's Word has the power to heal, deliver, and "prosper in the thing whereto He sends it." If we really believe that, then we will meditate on and speak His Word. God gave us His Word so we could prosper in life. We are not to hide the Word under a bushel and do nothing with it (Luke 11:33).

Some people fail to do with the Word what they're supposed to do because they're carrying condemnation from their past. But God sent His Word to those people too — to deliver them from that kind of thinking!

PHILIPPIANS 3:13
13 Brethren, I count not myself to have apprehended: but this one thing I do, FORGETTING THOSE THINGS WHICH ARE BEHIND, and reaching forth unto those things which are before.

Remember I said you've got to "lose" your mind or your natural way of thinking to become a success in God. Well, from reading this verse, you could say, "As far as your past is concerned, get a case of spiritual amnesia!" In effect, that's what this verse is saying: Forget what is behind you. Get hold of the mind of God concerning you and renew your mind — your old way of thinking. Then reach forward to the things of the future that God has in store for you — the things that He will give you as you conform *your* thoughts to *His* thoughts and learn to speak and act in line with His Word.

Some people say, "Well, I've seen some things in the Word that God wants me to have, but they just seem too big for me to obtain."

No one said anything about your obtaining God's best all by yourself. If you've been born again, you are in union with God. And nothing is too big or too hard for God (Jer. 32:27)!

You see, you and God together — the natural and the supernatural coming together — make an explosive force that can accomplish anything! Hallelujah!

Now look at the next verse in Philippians 3: *"I PRESS TOWARD the mark for the prize of the high calling of God in Christ Jesus"* (v. 14).

"To press toward" implies a person is doing something. He's not just sitting down, doing nothing.

Many people say, "Well, I'm just living by faith." But they're not really living by faith, because they're not doing anything. The Apostle Paul lived by faith by "getting with it" when it came to the things of God! Paul knew how to conform his thoughts to God's thoughts and then act on them. He didn't just sit idly by.

Say Good-Bye to the Past And Begin Moving With God!

I challenge you to purpose in your heart today to think God's thoughts in every situation and circumstance of life. No matter what comes your way, ask yourself, *What does the Word say about this?* Abandon your old way of thinking in the natural that has held you back from enjoying the blessings and benefits the Word promises.

Certainly, your natural mind will fight you. Your natural mind will tell you you're crazy — that you've lost your mind. But if you're thinking in line with God's Word, in the truest sense, you haven't lost your mind. You've "lost" your natural way of thinking and have gotten hold of *God's* thoughts. Now you're on the pathway to victory and success! Your impossibilities begin to fade into the background and become possibilities with God!

God's Word is what brings a person success in life. Blessed is the man who recognizes this fact and governs his life according to the Word!

Chapter 5

Blessed Is the Person Who Walks Closely With God

And Moses called unto Joshua, and said unto him in the sight of all Israel, Be strong and of a good courage: for thou must go with this people unto the land which the Lord hath sworn unto their fathers to give them; and thou shalt cause them to inherit it.

And the Lord, he it is that doth go before thee; he will be with thee, he will not fail thee, neither forsake thee: fear not, neither be dismayed . . . .

And the Lord said unto Moses, Behold, thy days approach that thou must die: call Joshua, and present yourselves in the tabernacle of the congregation, that I may give him a charge. And Moses and Joshua went, and presented themselves in the tabernacle of the congregation . . . .

And he gave Joshua the son of Nun a charge, and said, Be strong and of a good courage: for thou shalt bring the children of Israel into the land which I sware unto them: and I will be with thee.

— Deuteronomy 31:7,8,14,23

Moses was a man who was mightily used of God. Moses was God's chosen leader to deliver His people during the time of their captivity to Pharaoh in Egypt. It was Moses to whom God talked face to face (Exod. 33:11). God gave Moses instructions for the Israelites to follow in order to be delivered from Egypt and for their continued well-being and prosperity once they were delivered. I believe it is safe to say that Moses was someone who walked closely with God!

In the last part of Deuteronomy, it is recorded that Moses talked to Joshua and the others whom he'd led out of Egypt and Pharaoh's captivity. Moses knew that the end of his life was near, so he addressed Joshua in front of all the people of Israel, telling Joshua, "Be strong and of a good courage. Fear not; neither be dismayed" (Deut. 31:7,8).

After Moses died, the children of Israel mourned his death for thirty days. When the time of weeping and mourning had ended, the Bible says, *"And Joshua the son of Nun was full of the spirit of wisdom; for Moses had laid his hands upon him: and the children of Israel hearkened unto him, and did as the Lord commanded Moses"* (Deut. 34:9).

Notice that after the death of Moses, God gave Joshua practically the same exhortation He had given him before Moses died.

JOSHUA 1:5,6
5 There shall not any man be able to stand before thee all the days of thy life: as I was with Moses, so I will be with thee: I will not fail thee, nor forsake thee.
6 Be strong and of a good courage: for unto this people shalt thou divide for an inheritance the land, which I sware unto their fathers to give them.

This transferring of leadership from Moses to Joshua shows us something very interesting about God. After the Israelites had mourned the death of Moses thirty days, the Lord began moving them onward under the leadership of Joshua.

You see, God continually moves forward even when one of His servants dies. When one generation of servants passes off the scene, God moves on with a new generation. He never panics, and He is never anxious about whether or not His plan will be fulfilled.

Sometime in the early 1940s, Smith Wigglesworth and Aimee Semple McPherson, great ministers of the Gospel, went home to be with the Lord, and many Christians became anxious, hollering, "Oh, what are we going to do now! All of our great leaders are dying!"

But, you see, God will always raise up a new group of ministers, just as He raised up Joshua when Moses died. And that's the way it's been throughout the Bible. You can study the Bible from cover to cover and find that to be true.

Sure enough, in the 1940s when some of the leading ministers passed off the scene, God raised up some young ministers to continue heralding the Gospel of the Lord Jesus Christ.

Look to God, Not Man, For Answers

Friend, it's time we learned to look to the Word and to put our trust in God, not in man. Christians need never put their trust in what men can do to the extent they become anxious when those men pass off the scene.

On the other side of the coin, some "zealous" Charismatics have taught that the older ministers need to get out of the way so the younger ones can "come on the scene." That is just not so; it's a bunch of nonsense!

We can read the Bible and see that Joshua was on the scene under the leadership of Moses long before Moses died. Joshua remained in that position under Moses for a long time before it came time for Moses to pass on. Then God commanded Joshua to step up and take Moses' place.

Look again at Joshua chapter 1.

JOSHUA 1:1,2
1 Now after the death of Moses the servant of the Lord it came to pass, that the Lord spake unto Joshua the son of Nun, Moses' minister, saying,

2 Moses my servant is dead; now therefore arise, go over this Jordan, thou, and all this people, unto the land which I do give to them, even to the children of Israel.

Notice this passage *doesn't* say, "Now after the death of Moses, the servant of the Lord, it came to pass that the Lord *held a wake, and He mourned for forty days and forty nights and wondered who was going to lead His people*"!

No, God cannot be surprised, and He always has a plan! He never panics, and neither should we if we are following Him closely.

You see, Joshua had ministered to Moses when Moses was leader of the people of Israel. Moses "raised up" Joshua, so to speak. He trained Joshua.

In the Greek, the name "Joshua" is translated "Jesus," and there is some symbolism in the life of Joshua that points to the life of our Lord and Savior Jesus Christ. For example, Joshua was a deliverer; he led the children of Israel into the Promised Land after Moses had led them out of the bondage and slavery of Egypt.

Well, Jesus Christ is *the* Deliverer! He brought us out of the kingdom of darkness — out of bondage and slavery to sin. And once we are delivered, He leads us by His Spirit into our "promised land" — into the many blessings and benefits that He purchased for us in God's plan of redemption.

God Uses Those Who Walk Closely With Him

Joshua was a minister to Moses. Both men walked with God, and God used them to accomplish great things for His Kingdom. We could learn something today from these men. They were blessed because they walked with God. In other words, *blessed is the man who walks closely with God*!

I want you to realize that Joshua not only walked with God, but he was also *obedient* to Him. Joshua received his "marching orders" from God and moved or acted on those orders immediately. We can see this in Joshua 1:10.

JOSHUA 1:9-11
9 Have not I [the Lord] **commanded thee? Be strong and of a good courage; be not afraid, neither be thou dismayed: for the Lord thy God is with thee whithersoever thou goest.**
10 Then Joshua commanded the officers of the people, saying,
11 Pass through the host, and command the people, saying, Prepare you victuals; for within three days ye shall pass over this Jordan, to go in to possess the land, which the Lord your God giveth you to possess it.

In today's language, we could paraphrase verse 11: "Hey, guys, you've got three days to get everything packed, because we're moving out of here to cross the Jordan and go lay hold of what the Lord said belongs to us!"

Joshua told the people what the Lord had commanded him to tell them, knowing that these were the children of a very unbelieving bunch of Israelites. Their fathers had disobeyed Moses years before when they refused to go in and possess the land. So the Lord told Moses and Aaron that everyone twenty years old and older would die in the wilderness and not take possession of the Promised Land (Num. 14:26-35).

If you'll study the mathematics on this, you'll find that many people died during that forty-year period they were forced to wander in the wilderness because they had incurred God's wrath. Some of those people must have died awfully young. But, you see, unbelief and disobedience can cause a person to go to "sleep" early — to die prematurely.

However, the children of those who died in the wilderness were a completely different story. Since those twenty years old and older had died, the oldest people entering the Promised Land would have been just under sixty years old. When Joshua gave this generation their marching orders, notice what they did *not* say: "Aw, now wait a minute, Joshua! We need to do such-and-such first. We can't go into the Promised Land now."

No, the Bible says they were ready to go! They didn't appear to be fearful, unbelieving, or worried about anything!

We can learn something from this group of people that will help us walk and live in the blessings God has provided for us to have. Remember, we're talking about "blessed is the man or woman who walks closely with God."

To Walk Closely With God Is To Walk by *Faith*

In order to walk closely with God, we must walk by *faith*. The Bible says, *"But without faith it is impossible to please him: for he that cometh to God must believe that he is, and that he is a rewarder of them that diligently seek him"* (Heb. 11:6). And throughout the Word of God, we are told that the just shall live by faith (Hab. 2:4; Rom. 1:17; Gal. 3:11; Heb. 10:38). So, you see, in order to walk with God and please Him, we need to walk by faith. By faith in what? By faith in God's *Word*!

God has already provided many things for us, just as He provided the Promised Land to the children of Israel ahead of time. But we have to learn how to walk by faith to receive those things from Him.

In Joshua 1:3, we find a hint as to how to walk by faith and receive from God. Notice God tells Joshua to "tread upon" the land.

JOSHUA 1:3
3 Every place that the sole of your foot shall TREAD UPON, that have I given unto you, as I said unto Moses.

Notice God tells Joshua, *"Every place that the sole of your foot shall TREAD UPON . . . ."* Now you can't *tread* on something if you don't *walk* on it. So God was saying, in effect, "I've already given you the land. Now *you've* got to do something. You've got to get up and walk on it and take it by faith!"

In the New Testament, there are so many things that God has already given to us in Christ. But if we're going to *have* them — if we're going to take possession of those blessings — we're going to have to *do* something. We're going to have to get up and take them by faith!

Many people are sitting around, waiting passively for the blessings of God to come to them. But they need to get up and take those blessings by faith. They need to get moving for God, because when you're "sold out" and living wholeheartedly for God, the Bible says that *then* the blessings of God will overtake you (Deut. 28:2)! That means the blessings will come up from behind you, so to speak, and run you over!

The Bible doesn't say, "Just sit down and do nothing, and the blessings will overtake you." No, the blessings of God will overtake you *when you walk with God wholeheartedly* as Joshua and Caleb did (*see* Num. 32:12), and that means walking by faith!

The word "overtake" implies that something is coming from behind you. Well, the reason the blessings are going to come from *behind* you instead of from *in front of* you is that, as you're walking with God — treading upon the "land" or the blessing you are to possess — your feet haven't been in front of you yet! In other words, when it comes to receiving Bible promises, only that which you have treaded on by faith will become yours in reality!

Remember, God told Joshua, *"Every place that THE SOLE OF YOUR FOOT SHALL TREAD UPON, that have I given unto you, as I said unto Moses"* (Joshua 1:3). How in the world can you receive a particular blessing by "treading" on it if you haven't even gotten there yet! No, you've got to walk it out, claiming the blessing by faith as you're walking with and serving God wholeheartedly. Then as you continue moving with God, the blessings that you've already treaded on will overtake you!

Some people just want to automatically or instantly start walking in the blessings of God. But you have to start out walking by faith before you can progress. You've got to step out and put your foot of faith on the promises of God! *Then* you'll begin to enjoy Heaven's blessings!

The blessings will come up behind us as we're walking with God. And how did we say we are to walk with God? *By faith!* We have to walk by faith if we want the blessings of God to overtake us!

You Can Boldly Step Out On God's Word!

Have you ever watched someone cross a footbridge that he wasn't sure would hold him up? That person will usually grab hold of something else nearby for extra support and security.

One time when I was nine or ten years old, several of my friends and I were hiking through the woods and came up to a ravine we had to cross. Someone had sawed down a tree and placed it across the ravine. It was just a little tree, and we didn't know how strong it was — we didn't know whether it could support our weight as we crossed over.

Well, before we went running across that ravine, we wanted to make sure we were holding on to something else that we knew could support us, because there was about a fifty-foot drop to the bottom of the ravine!

We looked around and found a long pole that we could stick in the ground and hold on to as we crossed the ravine on that tree log. The pole was only long enough to hold on to part of the way across the ravine; then we had to let go of the pole and make a run for the other side!

I never will forget it. The first boy went across, and you could hear the log cracking as he stepped on it. When it was my turn, I "hit it running" and made it across. The last guy to cross just barely made it when — *crash* — the tree log went crumbling down to the bottom of the ravine! But we all made it, praise God! We made it safely to the other side.

That illustration could be compared to confidently stepping out "in" faith over the "ravines" of adverse circumstances, holding on to nothing but the Word of God. But there are a couple of differences to note. First, the Word of God is not like the cracking log placed across a ravine. God's Word is a solid Rock that you can confidently stand on; it will never crack, break, fall, or fail. When you're standing on the Word, the Word will never disappoint you or let you down.

Second, when you step out in faith on God's Word, you can't be tentative or unsure, as we were when we crossed that ravine. No, you've got to step out boldly, confidently, and with authority, because the enemy who's arrayed against you pays no attention to someone who is tentative. In fact, if you're not confident in what God's Word says about you, the enemy will "devour" you (1 Peter 5:8).

I see some people walking by faith the way someone might test the water in a swimming pool before diving in. Then there are others who take the "plunge of faith." Do you know what I mean by that? I mean, they believe God's Word wholeheartedly, and they take one big running leap into the "pool," claiming the blessings of God without wavering! Their feet are quick to tread on the ground of God's Word and His promises!

You know, the best way to get into a swimming pool full of cool water is just to jump in! All the testing in the world isn't going to change the temperature. In fact, getting in slowly may make you want to turn around and get out of the pool!

That is the way some people are with their faith. They're too tentative; they're not authoritative enough. Certainly, the situations and circumstances of life can be difficult. I'm not making light of tests and trials. But when all other ground is sinking sand — and others around you are going under — if you know what God has said in His Word and you're trusting Him, *you* won't go under! You'll be able to put the sole of your foot down and walk on solid ground, and you'll receive the blessing of God.

That reminds me of a story about three guys who were on a lake fishing in a boat near the shoreline. One of the fellows wanted a soft drink, so he stepped out of the boat and onto the shore to get the drink. The second guy wanted a soft drink, so he did the same thing. Then the third guy wanted a soft drink, but when he stepped out of the boat as the other two did, he sunk deep into the water. The first fellow looked at the second one and said, "I guess we should have told him where the rocks were"!

You see, when you're walking by faith, others around you may be "sinking" because they don't know where the "rocks" are! But you are standing tall; you are standing on the unmovable rock of God's Word! And you can walk on that Rock right on to victory! Wherever the sole of your foot shall tread by faith, the blessings of God will rise up and overtake you!

What I am saying is this: You must be prepared to take the venture of faith like Peter did in Matthew 14:25-29 when he stepped out on the water. You must be willing to step out onto the deep water with nothing under you but the Word of God! If Jesus says to you, "Walk," you must be willing to walk with nothing under you but His Word.

Yes, your faith will be tried. The Apostle Paul, who wrote more about faith in the New Testament than anyone else, was tried in his faith. But through every test and trial, Paul declared, "I always triumph!" (2 Cor. 2:14).

You see, when Paul studied at the feet of the great Rabbi Gamaliel, he studied his ancient forefathers — Moses, Abraham, Isaac, and Jacob. Paul knew what made them tick, so to speak. He knew about their faith in God.

We can learn a great deal from the experiences of the Old Testament men of faith, namely that there is nothing impossible to the one who believes and keeps on believing (Mark 9:23)!

One important key to faith is that we must act on God's Word *before* we see any change in our circumstances — while our situation remains the same. For example, in Joshua chapter 3 when the Lord instructed Joshua and the people to cross the Jordan River and move into the Promised Land, they had to obey the Lord in faith. Why? Because God didn't tell them He would part the waters of the Jordan *first* so they could cross over. No, He told the priests to proceed, and as soon as the soles of their feet "rested in the waters," *then* He would cause the river to be parted (v. 13). It was when the feet of the priests hit the water that the Jordan rolled back! That means the priests had to step out by faith!

Joshua 6:3-5 states the Lord commanded the children of Israel to march around the walls of Jericho seven times before blowing the trumpet. On the seventh day when the trumpets sounded, they were commanded to shout. *Then* the walls of Jericho fell down flat! God didn't tumble the walls *first*. He tumbled the walls *when they obeyed Him*, acting in faith on what He'd told them.

Trust God Over Natural Reasoning And Tumble Your 'Walls' of Defeat!

In other words, the children of Israel weren't shouting *because* God had tumbled the walls of Jericho and had given them the victory. No, they were shouting while the walls were still standing! They believed what God said — that the victory was already theirs!

All of us will face situations in life in which we must choose to believe God over what the circumstances are telling us. We must obey God and His Word even when it seems ridiculous to our mind to obey what He's telling us to do. To the natural mind, it doesn't seem intelligent to be worry-free when the storms of life are assailing. But if we want to come out of those storms victoriously, we must trust the Word of God over what our natural mind tells us.

In the case of the Israelites' victory over Jericho, it probably seemed like the most ridiculous thing they'd ever done in their lives — to march around the city seven times — as if marching around those walls was going to weaken them! No army in history had ever conquered the fortified city of Jericho. It has been said that Jericho's walls were so thick and wide that two chariots could drive side by side on top of them!

Anyone who knows anything about military strategy knows that you're not going to win a war and take a city just by marching around it! Yet that's exactly what God told the Israelites to do!

When the children of Israel obeyed God's command given through their leader Joshua, something happened on the seventh day when they were marching around the great city of Jericho for the seventh time.

JOSHUA 6:15,16,20
15 And it came to pass on the seventh day, that they rose early about the dawning of the day, and compassed the city after the same manner seven times: only on that day they compassed the city seven times.
16 And it came to pass at the seventh time, when the priests blew with the trumpets, Joshua said unto the people, Shout; for the Lord hath given you the city . . . .
20 So the people shouted when the priests blew with the trumpets: and it came to pass, when the people heard the sound of the trumpet, and the people shouted with a great shout, that the wall fell down flat, so that the people went up into the city, every man straight before him, and they took the city.

Before those walls fell, the Israelites had marched around the city six times, and nothing had happened; there wasn't so much as a crack in the wall!

The Israelites could have said, "We've been marching around these walls six times now. Surely if God was going to do something, He would have already done it. He would have at least *started* to do *something*. Surely these walls should already be crumbling." But they didn't say that. They obeyed God's instructions and won a mighty victory on the seventh day! They won the victory by their obedience and their faith!

Now I want you to understand that walking by faith is not always going to be easy. There will be obstacles in your way. For example, the Israelites had to first overcome the obstacle of the Jordan River and then Jericho to get to the Promised Land.

Then after Jericho was conquered, do you remember the battle at Ai recorded in the Book of Joshua?

Sin Short-Circuits the Blessings of God

First Corinthians 10:11 says that everything that happened to the children of Israel in the Old Testament was an example for us so that we would know how to live. We can look at what happened at Ai as an example of how *not* to live — in sin and disobedience! The story of the battle at Ai has its beginnings in the conquering of Jericho.

JOSHUA 6:16-19
16 And it came to pass at the seventh time, when the priests blew with the trumpets, Joshua said unto the people, Shout; for the Lord hath given you the city [of Jericho].
17 And THE CITY SHALL BE ACCURSED, even it, and all that are therein, to the Lord: only Rahab the harlot shall live, she and all that are with her in the house, because she hid the messengers that we sent.
18 And ye, in any wise KEEP YOURSELVES FROM THE ACCURSED THING, lest ye make yourselves

> **accursed, when ye take of the accursed thing, and make the camp of Israel a curse, and trouble it.**
> **19 But all the silver, and gold, and vessels of brass and iron, are consecrated unto the Lord: they shall come into the treasury of the Lord.**

You see, before the walls of Jericho fell, the children of Israel were given specific instructions about the spoils of Jericho. They were not to take anything from the city as spoils lest they make themselves accursed and bring trouble upon the whole camp of Israel.

We discussed in Chapter 3 that obedience is a key to your walking in God's blessings. Likewise, *dis*obedience is a sure way to cut yourself off from the blessings of God! But if you're walking closely with God, wholeheartedly, in intimate fellowship with Him, you won't walk in disobedience.

Read carefully the following passage of Scripture.

> **JOSHUA 7:1-12**
> **1 But the children of Israel COMMITTED A TRESPASS IN THE ACCURSED THING: for Achan, the son of Carmi, the son of Zabdi, the son of Zerah, of the tribe of Judah, took of the accursed thing: and the anger of the Lord was kindled against the children of Israel.**
> **2 And Joshua sent men from Jericho to Ai, which is beside Bethaven, on the east side of Bethel, and spake unto them, saying, Go up and view the country. And the men went up and viewed Ai.**
> **3 And they returned to Joshua, and said unto him, Let not all the people go up; but let about two or three thousand men GO UP AND SMITE AI; and**

make not all the people to labour thither; for they are but few.
4 So THERE WENT UP thither of the people ABOUT THREE THOUSAND MEN: AND THEY FLED BEFORE THE MEN OF AI.
5 And the men of Ai smote of them about thirty and six men: for they chased them from before the gate even unto Shebarim, and smote them in the going down: wherefore THE HEARTS OF THE PEOPLE MELTED, and became as water.
6 And Joshua rent his clothes, and fell to the earth upon his face before the ark of the Lord until the eventide, he and the elders of Israel, and put dust upon their heads.
7 And Joshua said, Alas, O Lord God, wherefore hast thou at all brought this people over Jordan, to deliver us into the hand of the Amorites, to destroy us? would to God we had been content, and dwelt on the other side Jordan!
8 O Lord, what shall I say, when Israel turneth their backs before their enemies!
9 For the Canaanites and all the inhabitants of the land shall hear of it, and shall environ us round, and cut off our name from the earth: and what wilt thou do unto thy great name?
10 And the Lord said unto Joshua, Get thee up; wherefore liest thou thus upon thy face?
11 ISRAEL HATH SINNED, and they have also transgressed my covenant which I commanded them: FOR THEY HAVE EVEN TAKEN OF THE ACCURSED THING, and have also stolen, and dissembled also, and they have put it even among their own stuff.
12 THEREFORE THE CHILDREN OF ISRAEL COULD NOT STAND BEFORE THEIR ENEMIES, but turned their backs before their enemies, BECAUSE THEY WERE ACCURSED: neither will I

be with you any more, except ye des
accursed from among you.

The Israelites were defeated at Ai, and the Lord revealed to Joshua that the reason they were defeated by their enemy was that there was disobedience in the camp.

JOSHUA 7:13-26
13 Up, sanctify the people, and say, Sanctify yourselves against to morrow: for thus saith the Lord God of Israel, There is an accursed thing in the midst of thee, O Israel: thou canst not stand before thine enemies, until ye take away the accursed thing from among you.
14 In the morning therefore ye shall be brought according to your tribes: and it shall be, that the tribe which the Lord taketh shall come according to the families thereof; and the family which the Lord shall take shall come by households; and the household which the Lord shall take shall come man by man.
15 And it shall be, that he that is taken with the accursed thing shall be burnt with fire, he and all that he hath: because he hath transgressed the covenant of the Lord, and because he hath wrought folly in Israel.
16 So Joshua rose up early in the morning, and brought Israel by their tribes; and the tribe of Judah was taken:
17 And he brought the family of Judah; and he took the family of the Zarhites: and he brought the family of the Zarhites man by man; and Zabdi was taken:
18 And he brought his household man by man; and Achan, the son of Carmi, the son of Zabdi, the son of Zerah, of the tribe of Judah, was taken.

19 And Joshua said unto Achan, My son, give, I pray thee, glory to the Lord God of Israel, and make confession unto him; and tell me now what thou hast done; hide it not from me.
20 And Achan answered Joshua, and said, Indeed I have sinned against the Lord God of Israel, and thus and thus have I done:
21 When I saw among the spoils a goodly Babylonish garment, and two hundred shekels of silver, and a wedge of gold of fifty shekels weight, then I coveted them, and took them; and, behold, they are hid in the earth in the midst of my tent, and the silver under it.
22 So Joshua sent messengers, and they ran unto the tent; and, behold, it was hid in his tent, and the silver under it.
23 And they took them out of the midst of the tent, and brought them unto Joshua, and unto all the children of Israel, and laid them out before the Lord.
24 And Joshua, and all Israel with him, took Achan the son of Zerah, and the silver, and the garment, and the wedge of gold, and his sons, and his daughters, and his oxen, and his asses, and his sheep, and his tent, and all that he had: and they brought them unto the valley of Achor.
25 And Joshua said, Why hast thou troubled us? the Lord shall trouble thee this day. And all Israel stoned him with stones, and burned them with fire, after they had stoned them with stones.
26 And they raised over him a great heap of stones unto this day. So the Lord turned from the fierceness of his anger. Wherefore the name of that place was called, The valley of Achor, unto this day.

After Joshua and the Israelites took care of the disobedience, the Lord told Joshua to go back to Ai, where they had previously been defeated. This time, God gave them a mighty victory (*see* Joshua chapter 8)!

In your own life, there may come a time when you feel the enemy has gained the upperhand and that God has forsaken you because of your disobedience. Well, if that happens, that doesn't mean God has forsaken you, because He hasn't. No, check up on yourself, ask for forgiveness, and get back on the road of obedience to God and His Word. You'll be blessed as you do, because blessed is the man or woman who walks closely with God.

Chapter 6

Purpose and Courage: Two Ingredients for Walking In the Fullness of God

As I said previously, we are to learn something from the experiences of the Israelites. One thing we are to learn is the importance of walking closely with God by faith. But not only did the children of Israel walk by faith to possess the Promised Land — they also walked with *purpose*.

You've got to keep your purpose in mind when you're walking with God. Many people claim to be walking by faith, but they're just walking. They don't have a clear vision before them of what God wants them to have or what He wants them to do.

The Israelites weren't just walking. They had a divine purpose for every step they took. Every step where the soles of their feet trod was a step of purpose! What was the purpose? It was to take what God said already belonged to them (Josh. 1:1-9).

You and I today also need to keep our focus and sense of purpose as we're walking with God. Without that sense of purpose — that vision or goal set before us — we will end up defeated on the road of life.

Even in the natural, a person has to have purpose before he can succeed. Everyone needs a goal that he desires to accomplish. His goal is what he sets before him to keep him going when the going gets rough. Unless he keeps his sense of purpose, he'll end up quitting during the hard times.

Hold Fast to Your God-Given Purpose or Goal

Your sense of God-given purpose will also give you the confidence you need to fulfill your goal. Whatever God tells you to do, you can do it with the knowledge that He is with you every step of the way.

> **JOSHUA 1:5**
> **5 There shall not any man be able to stand before thee all the days of thy life: as I was with Moses, so I will be with thee: I will not fail thee, nor forsake thee.**

When you begin the walk of faith, you have to have this same confidence that Joshua had. God said, "*. . . I will not fail thee, nor forsake thee.*" You have to be confident of the victory before you ever start to attain it. You have to be confident that, through Christ, you can do all things. You have to be confident in God's Word and continue walking by faith when it looks as if nothing is happening.

When you're walking by faith with God and your confidence is in Him, you can hold your head high and keep right on walking, even when tests and trials are assailing. You see, your confidence is not in the things around you, but in the everlasting Word of God.

We see an example of this kind of confidence in the New Testament in the case of the Apostle Peter. When Jesus walked on the water and came to the disciples' boat, the disciples were frightened; they thought they were seeing a ghost. Then Peter said, "*. . . Lord, if it be thou, bid me come unto thee on the water*" (Matt. 14:28). Jesus said to Peter, "Come!" and Peter stepped out of the boat, confident in Jesus' word to him (v. 29).

As long as Peter kept his eyes on Jesus, he walked on the water with the Lord. But when Peter began to look at the circumstances around him — the boisterous wind and the waves — he began to sink (v. 30).

Similarly, if you begin to focus your attention on your circumstances instead of upon Jesus, you're going to do what Peter did; you'll begin to "sink." You've got to keep your eyes on Jesus and His Word, because that is what will see you through to victory.

Friend, the circumstances of life come to us all; no one is exempt. And the circumstances may scream at you, *You won't make it! You can't accomplish this goal. You won't make it through this trial. You don't have the ability. You don't have the finances. Look at your symptoms. The doctor's prognosis isn't very good.* But when you are faced with those thoughts, you have to hold on to your sense of purpose and have the confidence that "*. . . all things are possible to him that believeth*" (Mark 9:23)!

Jesus said, "*. . . In the world ye shall have tribulation: but be of good cheer; I have overcome the world*" (John 16:33).

Courage: The Second Ingredient

Besides *purpose*, there is another ingredient to add to your walking closely with God, and that is *courage*.

> **JOSHUA 1:6,7**
> **6 Be strong and of a GOOD COURAGE: for unto this people shalt thou divide for an inheritance the land, which I sware unto their fathers to give them.**
> **7 Only be thou strong and very COURAGEOUS, that thou mayest observe to do according to all the law, which Moses my servant commanded thee: turn not from it to the right hand or to the left, that thou mayest prosper whithersoever thou goest.**

It takes courage to walk with God by faith. It takes courage to move out against the unknown with the Word of God as your only support. When you can hardly see a step in front of you, so to speak, you have to take hold of the hand of the One who sees everything clearly.

That's what the children of Israel did in possessing their Promised Land. And that's what you're going to have to do if you want to possess the blessings God has already provided for you.

Don't Let Fear Rob You of Success in Life

It takes courage to step out and do what God has told you to do, because, oftentimes, what God tells you to do is not logical.

For example, I know of ministers who bought Gospel tents because the Lord told them to. Some of these preachers took them into sections of cities that most people would be afraid to minister in — areas devastated by poverty, drugs, race riots, and gangs.

It takes courage to walk up to a gang leader and say, "You need Jesus." You've got to really believe what you say you believe! You've got to have confidence in God and His Word. You can't just read scriptures one time to have this confidence; you've got to have them deeply rooted and firmly established in your heart. And that comes through meditating in the Word.

JOSHUA 1:8
8 This book of the law shall not depart out of thy mouth; but thou shalt MEDITATE THEREIN DAY AND NIGHT, that thou mayest observe to do according to all that is written therein: for then thou shalt make thy way prosperous, and then thou shalt have good success.

The reason many people have never received anything from the Lord is that they're afraid to step out and walk by faith to receive it. They are comfortable walking by sight rather than walking by something they can't see or feel. But to receive from God, you need to have the attitude, *Bless God, His Word is true. I believe it, and that settles it. I can receive what I need from God.*

PHILIPPIANS 4:13
13 I can do all things through Christ which strengtheneth me.

Our problem is, so many times we start talking about what we *can't* do, instead of what we *can* do through Christ! Therefore, we are defeated by our thoughts before we ever get to the battle!

It would do you good to say Philippians 4:13 out loud regularly: "I can do all things through Christ who strengthens me." Then let it be your confidence; let it be your courage to go out and do what God's Word says you can do.

The Importance of A Positive Attitude

I remember a little 165-pound guard who played on a high school football team in Garland, Texas, in the early 1960s. They'd won two state championships back to back. Then they came up against a team from Fort Worth, Texas.

The 165-pound guard was going to have to play against a 278-pound defensive tackle. This defensive tackle for Fort Worth had previously devastated everyone he'd played against on the field.

The coach for the Garland team began to pump up that little 165-pound guard. He showed the player film clips of the Fort Worth defensive tackle and made comments, such as: "See how slow this guy is? Look how slow he is!"

Then the coach began to tell the little guard, "You're quick. In fact, you're so quick, you could get under that big fellow, hit him in the legs, and take him to the ground before he ever even gets moving!" The coach showed his man all of his opponent's faults and shortcomings, and then the coach exhorted the little guard about all the things he *could* do that the big guy *couldn't* do. You see, instead of telling his player, "You can't overpower that big defensive tackle; you're not strong enough," the coach told him what he *could* do!

The Garland coach pumped up his guard so much that when game day came, the other team had to take their defensive tackle out of the game in the middle of the third quarter! That little 165-pound kid hit that defensive tackle from all sides, *because he believed he could do it*!

Interviewers spoke with the tackle later, and he was still breathing hard. He told the interviewers, "That little guard was too quick. I would look for him, and the next thing I knew, he was taking my feet right from under me."

How did that happen? I believe it happened because Garland's coach had built confidence in that kid — not by telling him what he *couldn't* do, but by telling him what he *could* do!

Let the Word Dispel The Enemy's Lies

Do you understand my point? When it comes to your everyday life, you've got to believe and have confidence in God's Word. Let His Word "pump you up." Then when you come face to face with a challenge, you'll have the courage to withstand it fearlessly, knowing that the victory belongs to you and that you can do all things through Christ who strengthens you!

Of course, in order to do that, you'll have to quit listening to the devil's lies and to all your unbelieving friends and relatives who will be quick to tell you what you can't do. Your friends and family may mean well, but if you listen to them, you'll be defeated. You need to listen to God; He won't tell you what you *can't* do. He will tell you what you *can* do, and He'll give you the power and the strength to do it!

Faith Demands Action

However, you must believe what God tells you and have the courage to act on it. There are many people who say they believe God. But there is a difference between believing and actually executing or carrying out what you believe. It's as you step out and start to move that the supernatural power of God takes over and enables you to win the victory.

Many people are waiting for the power of God to overtake them so they can move out to stand against the devil. But that's not how God works. The Bible says, "Whatever *you put your hand to* shall prosper" (Deut. 23:20; Ps. 1:3). Some are waiting around for God to overtake them and move their hand *for* them! No, if they get up and do something, *then* the Lord will bless them.

"Yes," someone said. "But I'm just not sure God will meet me when I step out." But, you see, that's where meditation in the Word comes in. Meditation in the Word brings confidence in God and His Word. You've got to be confident that God's strength will come upon you as you step out.

In the Old Testament, God endowed Samson with extraordinary *physical* strength, yet it was supernatural strength (*see* Judges chapters 13-16). Samson did all the exploits he did, not in his own strength, but through the strength of the Lord. You see, Samson had to believe something when he picked up the jawbone of that donkey and began to swing it (Judges 15:15,16). Then when Samson began to take the first swing in his own power, the supernatural power of God took over, and mighty exploits were performed!

We know that Samson operated in God's strength and not his own. Why do I say that? Because after Samson revealed to Delilah the secret of his God-given strength, the power of the Lord departed from him, and Samson became as any other man. He was no longer able to conquer a thousand men single-handedly as he had done before (Judges 16:17)!

JUDGES 16:18-21
18 And when Delilah saw that he had told her all his heart, she sent and called for the lords of the Philistines, saying, Come up this once, for he hath shewed me all his heart. Then the lords of the Philistines came up unto her, and brought money in their hand.
19 And she made him sleep upon her knees; and she called for a man, and she caused him to shave off the seven locks of his head; and she began to afflict him, and his strength went from him.
20 And she said, The Philistines be upon thee, Samson. And he awoke out of his sleep, and said, I will go out as at other times before, and shake

myself. And he wist not that the Lord was departed from him.
21 But the Philistines took him, and put out his eyes, and brought him down to Gaza, and bound him with fetters of brass; and he did grind in the prison house.

If you'll read further, you'll find that after Samson became a prisoner of the Philistines, he repented before the Lord, and the Lord gave Samson back his strength to perform one last exploit.

JUDGES 16:23-30
23 Then the lords of the Philistines gathered them together for to offer a great sacrifice unto Dagon their god, and to rejoice: for they said, Our god hath delivered Samson our enemy into our hand.
24 And when the people saw him, they praised their god: for they said, Our god hath delivered into our hands our enemy, and the destroyer of our country, which slew many of us.
25 And it came to pass, when their hearts were merry, that they said, Call for Samson, that he may make us sport. And they called for Samson out of the prison house; and he made them sport: and they set him between the pillars.
26 And Samson said unto the lad that held him by the hand, Suffer me that I may feel the pillars whereupon the house standeth, that I may lean upon them.
27 Now the house was full of men and women; and all the lords of the Philistines were there; and there were upon the roof about three thousand men and women, that beheld while Samson made sport.
28 And Samson called unto the Lord, and said, O Lord God, remember me, I pray thee, and strengthen me, I pray thee, only this once, O God,

> **that I may be at once avenged of the Philistines for my two eyes.**
> **29 And Samson took hold of the two middle pillars upon which the house stood, and on which it was borne up, of the one with his right hand, and of the other with his left.**
> **30 And Samson said, Let me die with the Philistines. And he bowed himself with all his might; and the house fell upon the lords, and upon all the people that were therein. SO THE DEAD WHICH HE SLEW AT HIS DEATH WERE MORE THAN THEY WHICH HE SLEW IN HIS LIFE.**

What made the difference between Samson's life as a Philistine prisoner and this mighty act of vengeance upon God's enemies? It was the power of God! Samson's repentance brought the power of God back into his life. And if we walk closely with God, we will have the power of God in our lives, too, to do whatever He has called *us* to accomplish for Him.

Confidence in God's Word and Power Will Make Weakness a Thing of the Past

It may sound like a ridiculous comparison, but Samson's life without the power of God was sort of like the cartoon figure Popeye without his spinach! In the cartoon, the spinach empowered Popeye. Without the spinach, Popeye was weak, and Brutus, the bully, would beat him up. However, as soon as Popeye ate a can of spinach, his muscles would begin to bulge, and he'd lift Brutus in midair as if his enemy was a stick in the wind!

Similarly, when the enemy of our soul comes against us, we are going to have to stand our ground against him by faith. When we do, the Spirit of God will come on us, and we'll enforce Satan's defeat as if his power were nothing but a dry, brittle stick!

But it will take courage and confidence in God and His Word to accomplish this. Look again at one of our main scripture texts.

JOSHUA 1:9
9 Have not I commanded thee? Be strong and of a good courage; be not afraid, neither be thou dismayed: for the Lord thy God is with thee whithersoever thou goest.

That goes right along with a New Testament verse of Scripture.

HEBREWS 13:5
5 . . . I [the Lord] **will never leave thee, nor forsake thee.**

What does that mean to the believer? It means that through the good and the bad and the "thick and the thin," the Lord is there! When you feel as if He's there and when you *don't* feel as if He's there, *He is there*! He will never leave you, nor forsake you.

The Lord Is *With* You!

So no matter what the situation or circumstance, you can be confident that the Lord is with you! Some people only feel confident and courageous when they're in a service where there is corporate faith. They feel good, they're excited about the things of God, and their confidence soars! But you can overcome the tests and trials of life, not only when you feel good, but when you feel as low as the floor under your feet! Why? Because God said He would never leave you nor forsake you (Heb. 13:5)!

Given the fact that God will never leave you, all you need to do is believe and confess, "I can do all things through Christ who strengthens me. I can accomplish this task through the power of God!"

You can probably recall the story of "the little train that *could*." Faced with an overwhelming task, the little train kept on saying, "I think I can. I think I can." And do you know what — he *could*! He could, because he *believed* he could.

It all comes back to what you believe. God's Word says that He will meet all of your needs according to His riches in glory. Therefore, the "sole of your foot" can tread confidently on the territory of prosperity.

If you will "walk not" in the counsel of the ungodly and walk closely with God by faith, you will find that there is no defeat in Christ Jesus! Every blessing that God has provided for you in Christ is yours! Through meditating in God's Word, you can have the courage and confidence you need to tread on and possess the promised blessings that belong to you. You can have success and victory in life, walking in all the fullness of God!

About the Author

Kenneth Hagin Jr., Executive Vice-President of Kenneth Hagin Ministries and Pastor of RHEMA Bible Church, teaches from a rich and diversified background of more than thirty-five years in the ministry.

Rev. Hagin Jr. attended Southwestern Assemblies of God College and graduated from Oral Roberts University with a degree in religious education. He also holds an honorary Doctor of Divinity degree from Faith Theological Seminary in Tampa, Florida.

After serving as an associate pastor, Rev. Hagin Jr. traveled as an evangelist throughout the United States and abroad and was responsible for organizing RHEMA Bible Training Center, a school which equips men and women for the ministry.

In addition to his administrative and teaching responsibilities at RHEMA, Rev. Hagin Jr. is pastor of RHEMA Bible Church, a large, thriving congregation on the RHEMA campus. He is also International Director of RHEMA Ministerial Association International, has a weekly radio program, "RHEMA Radio Church," which is heard on stations throughout the United States, and a television program, "RHEMA Praise."

Faith Library Publications Favorites

To order any of these books or for a complete listing of our Faith Library books, audio and video tapes, and music tapes and CDs, please call:

(918) 258-1588, ext. 2224

WELCOME TO GOD'S FAMILY: A Foundational Guide for Spirit-Filled Living

Kenneth E. Hagin • Item #528

Increase your spiritual effectiveness by discovering what it means to be born again and how you can partake of the biblical benefits that God has provided for you as His child!

BLESSED IS...Untying the 'NOTS' That Hinder Your Blessing!

Kenneth Hagin Jr. • Item #735

This book creatively teaches believers from Psalm 1 what *not* to do in order to be blessed by God and receive His richest and best!

GOD'S WORD: A Never-Failing Remedy

Kenneth E. Hagin • Item #526

The never-failing remedy for every adversity of life can be found in the pages of God's holy written Word! And when you act on the Word, it truly becomes a never-failing remedy!

ANOTHER LOOK AT FAITH

Kenneth Hagin Jr. • Item #733

This book focuses on what faith is not, thus answering common misunderstandings of what it means to live by faith.

THE BELIEVER'S AUTHORITY

Kenneth E. Hagin • Item #406

Our all-time best-seller, this book provides excellent insight into the authority that rightfully belongs to every believer in Christ!

DON'T QUIT! YOUR FAITH WILL SEE YOU THROUGH

Kenneth Hagin Jr. • Item #724

Learn how you can develop faith that won't quit and come out of tests or trials victoriously.

FOLLOWING GOD'S PLAN FOR YOUR LIFE

Kenneth E. Hagin • Item #519

It's up to individual Christians to fulfill the divine purpose that God ordained for their lives before the beginning of time. This book can help believers stay on the course God has set before them!

HEALING: Forever Settled

Kenneth Hagin Jr. • Item #723

The primary question among believers is whether it's God's will to heal people today. Healing is a forever-settled subject because God's Word is forever settled!

HOW TO LIVE WORRY-FREE

Kenneth Hagin Jr. • Item #735

Sound teaching from God's Word is combined with practical insights to illustrate the perils of worry and to help guide the believer into the peace of God.

HOW YOU CAN BE LED BY THE SPIRIT OF GOD

Kenneth E. Hagin • Item #513

These step-by-step guidelines based on the Scriptures can help Christians avoid spiritual pitfalls and follow the Spirit of God in every area of life.

IT'S YOUR MOVE!

Kenneth Hagin Jr. • Item #730

Move out of the arena of discouragement and despair and into the arena of God's blessings that are yours in Christ.

LOVE: The Way To Victory

Kenneth E. Hagin • Item #523

By acting on the truths contained in this book, believers can turn around seemingly impossible situations in their lives — just by walking in the God-kind of love!

THE TRIUMPHANT CHURCH

Kenneth E. Hagin • Item #520

This best-seller is a comprehensive biblical study of the origin and operation of Satan that shows believers how to enforce his defeat in their lives.

THE UNTAPPED POWER IN PRAISE

Kenneth Hagin Jr. • Item #725

The power of God is available to set believers free. This book teaches how to tap into that power through praise!

WHAT TO DO WHEN FAITH SEEMS WEAK & VICTORY LOST

Kenneth E. Hagin • Item #501

The ten steps outlined in this book can bring any believer out of defeat into certain victory!